The First Book in the S

Reflections on the struggles of adoption and mental health and the strengths found along the way

Mysterious Ways

HEATHER GROTH

credo
house publishers

Other books in the *Struggles and Strengths* Series
Purpose for the Pain
God Loves You

Mysterious Ways
Copyright © 2020 by Heather Groth
All rights reserved.

Published in the United States by Credo House Publishers, a division of Credo Communications LLC, Grand Rapids, Michigan. credohousepublishers.com

ISBN: 978-1-62586-153-5

Cover and interior design by Frank Gutbrod
Editing by Donna Huisjen

Printed in the United States of America
First edition

Contents

Preface

"You are a saint." *Saint.* I cringe at the word. Saint is what many people try calling me when they find out that I adopted a sibling group of three school-aged children. I have made plenty of mistakes in my life, especially in the last few years with the children. I guess that is what parenting is all about, trial and error.

I originally began journaling just for me. It was just to get my thoughts and feelings out. I did not intend for my life to be an open book. However, as I continue to watch myself grow closer to God and realize new strengths, I recognize (or God has told me) that others could benefit from my life actually being an open book.

Everything in this book is true, based on my perception. No events have been altered or changed for the reader's benefit. These events did happen, and these are my true feelings at the time they took place. There was a time when I stopped journaling my feelings, but I recap how I was generally feeling at the time. Names and locations have been changed to protect the identity of all.

Everyone has the ability to influence lives. We are all an important piece of the puzzle called life. There is no villain in my memoir series. If you read this and figure out you are a character in my memoir, notice when the event took place and reflect how you may have grown closer to God or have changed. You will see through this memoir series that I have changed and grown. That is a very important piece of life—changing and growing into who we are meant to be.

If you read this and recognize who we are, please do not share this knowledge. My purpose in writing has nothing to do with recognition, applause, or the divulging of insider information. This book is strictly a tool from God to help those in need. I hope something in this lights a spark for you to grow closer to God because He works in "Mysterious Ways," always has a "Purpose for the Pain," and "God Loves You."

CHAPTER 1

Helpless

October 14, 2013

I anxiously fidgeted at the kitchen table while I listened to my kids' story underlining why police are bad and untrustworthy. As the anxiety ate at my stomach like a hungry monster, I picked at the crumbs on the table that were left over from our freshly eaten dinner. The table was still covered in dishes and some uneaten food. Over time I have learned to take whatever moments I can when the kids decide to open up about their past life before we adopted them.

The kids' story had taken place a few years prior to our adopting them. They had been at the home of their father, Chad, cooking dinner with his then current girlfriend, when their mother showed up, very angry.

"Mom was angry that dad had a girlfriend," Erica remembered, "even though Mom and Dad weren't together."

Of the three children, I figured Erica had the most insight because she is the oldest and remembers events from their past most vividly.

"Yeah, she came in and attacked Chad with a fork!" exclaimed Kayla.

"NO, it was a knife!" scolded Erica.

Erica corrected the other two as they shared their perspective on the story. Even Ethan, the youngest, tended to get scolded for throwing in his two cents because he would have been too young to remember. Poor Ethan. He was always being told that he wouldn't remember because he was too young when those past events happened.

My stomach churned at the picture the three kids painted. It was a very choppy story coming from the mouths of the twelve-, nine-, and seven-year-olds we had adopted a year earlier.

"After Mom tried to stab Dad, his girlfriend took us outside and called the police," Erica reported. "We got put in the police car when they came."

"It was scary," Ethan chimed in.

"SSHHHH!" Kayla hissed at Ethan.

"We watched Mom come out of the house and the police attacked her. They wrestled her down to the ground and stuck her with a needle," Erica continued.

"Yeah, then they put her in an ambulance. There were so many lights flashing—red, blue, . . . white." Kayla recalled.

Ethan exclaimed, "That was the last time I saw her!" Kayla, the nine-year-old, scolded him again: "NO, IT WASN'T. We saw her at Grandma's house." "The needle was huge! It was really long and they stuck it into her arm," Erica cut in.

The three kids were all in a chatter, each with their different version of what had happened. My husband and I just listened.

From what I understand from the children's family members and the DHS paperwork, their mom was high on meth. The needle must have been an injection to bring her down from her high. Their dad and mom were by then divorced but were still seeing each other on the side.

From this incident forward the children had continued to view the police as bad. They did not understand why their mother had been so angry or why the police had to wrestle her to the ground to inject her with a needle. Now Erica panicked every time she saw flashing lights or police cars.

Being that Erica is the oldest, the other two idolized her. They saw Erica as the leader, or even as their mom. Therefore, if Erica thought that police are bad, so did they.

"That's why I don't like police," Erica finished. "They attacked my mom. They don't try to keep you safe. They are bad."

We finished up from dinner and started the bedtime routines. It was Kayla's shower night, so I sent her to the bathroom while Erica went to her bedroom to read. Ethan ran for the living room to catch a little bit of TV. My husband, Scott, joined Ethan in the living room.

I liked that the living room was just a few steps down from the kitchen. Being it was a multi-level house, it was easy to see into the living room from the kitchen. It made me feel relief being able to keep an eye on the interaction between Scott and Ethan.

Dinner was becoming more stressful than enjoyable. I had always thought dinner should be a time for a family to get together to discuss their day and enjoy each other's company. Scott viewed it more as a formal thing.

He believed, "There should be no elbows on the table. Use utensils appropriately. Use your manners."

I agreed on principle. Meals should not be eaten like animals, but they should also be enjoyable. Scott took these issues of etiquette to another level and enforced them so strictly that it caused stress for all of us. Especially Ethan.

"Stop eating like a pig. Hold your fork the right way. Close your mouth when you chew. It's disgusting." Scott would nag at him at almost every meal.

Frustrated over many of the turns of events in my life, I decided that I would compose a Word document. I wanted to record my memories and feelings on the computer because my writing journal was being tapped into. Someone else's eyes were violating the thoughts and expressions I had been documenting. I wanted to journal but was afraid of so many eyes, young and old alike.

Yes, I would resort to the relative privacy of the computer to get my thoughts out. That way I could clear the screen quickly from prying eyes. That way no one else would have access.

I joined the boys in the living room with the laptop. One by one the girls joined us too, and we all sat in silence on our giant sectional. I purposely sat further away from Scott this evening so I could type without his looking over my shoulder. The kids zoned out— or perhaps I should say zoned *into* the TV—as they did nearly every night, and we sat quietly while my husband's favorite show was on.

I begin to type:

Journal Entry

I need to get a few things off my chest. With no one to talk to, I am hoping this will work. My major stress is Scott's constant yelling every day. He's always after Ethan about everything. Granted, Ethan can get under my skin, too, but his counselor is starting to believe that he has ADHD. We are getting him tested. Scott needs to have a little patience. I don't have patience lately either. If only I felt better. The kids seem depressed.

Erica called Scott's yelling out today to me. Saying that it is embarrassing when he yells in public and everyone is looking at them.

"It's not that bad," I say. But is it? Do I keep sticking my head in the sand like nothing is going on?

I notice his anger, some days more than others, but I do love Scott. I know the kids do too. Erica gets so mad about his yelling, yet she still goes to him with her problems, not me. I know this is because I am the mother figure and I am from her perspective invading her territory. Maybe I'm overreacting.

We met my sister's boyfriend's family for the first time over the weekend. We went to their house out of state. Erica said that the boyfriend's mom came to her crying over the weekend.

Erica said the mom told her, "Someone needs to talk to Scott about his yelling. It isn't right."

Scott was out of line again. I think it is the stress of traveling that makes him like that. Yet he gets like that at home too, especially when he can't control everyone or communicate what he wants. Maybe it's lack of communication or stress.

We're all stressed that I don't feel well. I just have to feel better right now, be over this and be all better, at least to everyone else.

I am angry at this mom for bringing her concern to Erica. If she had a problem she should have brought it to me, not a twelve-year-old girl with her own anger issues. Should I confront this mom? I'm not even sure the report is true. Why would she have been crying?

She isn't the first person to address this issue. Even the kids' birth grandma, Abigail, has talked to Scott about his anger. My mom, my sister, and my church friend have all expressed concerns. What do I do? If I mention to him about cooling off it always causes a fight.

Scott's motto: "I am just going to be the prick, and I don't care what others think of me. These kids need hard discipline. As long as they grow up to be functioning adults in society, then I have done my job."

Every child needs discipline, but to a point where they are scared of you? Then we have our good moments too. I question our decision to take on these kids. It has been very stressful.

I find that the kids use people to their advantage. They seem to know what they want from someone, and they will get it. Maybe this is a method of survival.

I feel that our marriage is suffering, and I have changed as a person also. I'm not as happy as I used to be. I have even noticed this when I am with my daycare kids. I'm irritable—it could be from not feeling well. Then again the not feeling well could be stress. There are days where I think about a divorce. Where would we go? What would I do? What kind of message would that send to the kids? I do love Scott, and we have our good moments too.

It's not as though he'll physically hurt us, but the verbal can be just as bad. No, he won't get physical. If he does we're gone in a heartbeat. Not going through that again. I guess I will keep sticking my head in the sand because I am used to getting yelled at. I suffered at the hands of physical abuse, so yelling is nothing. I should be thankful.

I am not scared of Scott's temper because it pales in comparison to my ex-fiancé's—well, I guess it is close. The kids are not used to getting yelled at, so I need to be their advocate. Do I love the kids as much as I do Scott? I had him first.

The kids cause a lot of stress and act as though they hate us. Yet we have our good times too. I feel that adoption isn't the same situation as having your own, yet everyone I try to talk to about our problems says it is the same. It's as though other parents who haven't adopted before just don't understand.

"The kids just need a lot of love," is what I hear a lot from others. I feel like I am getting drained like a sink that has a slow leak while you wash dishes. You try to fill the sink back up, but every time you turn on the faucet there is nothing there. What if I can't get the dishes cleaned?

The kids have baggage—they have seen a lot of traumatic things, have feelings of abandonment, and have a history of family mental illness. If they were our own, we wouldn't have half of these problems. Thank God we are with counselors who are seeing these illnesses in both girls and can give us tools to cope. We knew going into the adoption that the kids were going to have baggage, but we had no idea about the mental illnesses.

I closed the laptop and zoned out into the TV. I felt better venting to the computer, even though it wouldn't respond back. I watched the people move about the TV screen but did not hear a word they said. My thoughts drifted to the past, to how I had thought it was going to be, and then forward to how I was going to save these kids!

CHAPTER 2

The Beginning

In my opinion, my childhood could have been more pleasant. However, I have learned that I a lot of people feel that way. As parents you try your best to give your child the world, but somewhere along the way you start filling a jar with issues for their future counseling because we are only human. Looking back now, I realize that my childhood experiences made me into who I am today, and I wouldn't change it for the world.

Growing up on a farm in small-town Iowa, I didn't have a personal relationship with God. He was something or someone you feared. God was not my friend, and He was not a savior. We went to church every Sunday, but for some reason I didn't want a relationship with Him.

I lived in a godless world during my college years and into my mid twenties, going from one bed to another and drinking myself into oblivion. Eventually I decided that I wanted to grow up, leave the party life, and have a family.

2006

I met Scott through my cousin. He lived in Nebraska, but both our families lived in the same Iowa community. Scott is a diabetic and had multiple kidney transplants prior to our relationship. He had a rough life taking care of himself. I felt as though he needed help, and that I needed to be a caregiver.

As of today, I still don't know what it was about Scott that I liked. Maybe it was the truck he drove, or the thrill of getting away from a small town and moving to a city. At the time I really thought I wanted to settle down and have kids with him.

2007

I moved to Omaha, Nebraska, away from my friends and family in Iowa. I found a good paying, full-time job at a local daycare. We decided to purchase a townhouse together. It was a brand new housing development. I really felt grown up being able to purchase a place that was brand new.

We went to the closing table, and Scott had me convinced that he had everything taken care of. After looking at our credit, the financial institution representative came back from the back room.

"Scott, your credit is not good. You are too high of a risk. However, we ran Heather's credit too. She has excellent credit. You won't need a down payment if you only put the house in her name."

Scott was furious. I remember looking out the window and thinking, *We only have $1,000 good grace money down. We can walk away.*

Scott and I talked it over. He helped us come to the decision that we really wanted the house. I felt prestigious and needed. We settled down in our new house with our rat terrier, Harley. Harley is a spitfire of energy. He loves to play and brings me a lot of joy.

2008

We got married and immediately tried to have kids because I wanted them so badly. We went about our mundane lives going to work, shopping, and spending time together. We went back to our home area frequently to see his family and occasionally mine. We camped and canoed in the summer and snowmobiled in the winter.

CHAPTER 3

Needing a Change

Spring 2010

After a few years of our mundane life, I wanted more. There was something missing in my life. I was not sure what it was. There was a void that I needed to fill. I was tired of being in a rut. I was unhappy.

I was also homesick. I wanted to move back to Iowa and my home area. I was wanting to go back to the farm life, not caring for the city life. Whenever I brought it up to Scott it was always the same answer: *"If you can find me a job that pays as much as I get paid here, then we will move back."*

My coworker introduced me to a series of books. These books were about God and the end times. I started reading them with a little skepticism. Soon I discovered that I couldn't put them down. I filled myself with new information and experienced a hunger for more. I started talking to myself, which turned into conversations with the mysterious God. I soon found myself having little gut instincts, although I was terrified to follow them. I didn't know whether this was truly Him talking *to* me or the words were just in my head. Spurred by this newfound love, I found a local church just down the street. We started to attend regularly.

We were having problems conceiving children. Based on all the medications Scott had to take to avoid rejecting his kidney, we assumed that he was the reason we couldn't have kids. We decided to adopt, hoping that by word of mouth we could find a baby.

January 2011

I woke up to my cell phone ringing downstairs. I reached down to grab it but missed the call. It was my dad. I saw that I had missed thirteen calls from him during the night. I knew something bad had happened.

I quickly called him back. "Heather, we were in a terrible car accident last night," my dad said hastily. "Your brother and I suffered concussions, but your mom is in really bad shape. She is going into surgery soon." I quickly left to be with my family in Iowa.

My mom had suffered damage to all four of her limbs, along with a major cut on her neck from her seat belt, and had internal bleeding. They did surgery to remove her spleen. My mom would be in the hospital for three solid months, as she wouldn't be able to move any of her limbs.

February 2011

While my mom was in the hospital, she visited with a lot of doctors. Through word of mouth we were able to find a mother who wanted to give up her baby for adoption. She was already the mother of four children, all with different fathers, and another was going to be too much. We met with her at the ultrasound. It was a little girl! I had always dreamt of having a little girl! She was due in May, so we had very little time to prepare. I was ecstatic! The mysterious God was answering my prayers!

The planning began, along with picking out names and starting to gather baby stuff. How exciting! During this time the birth mom wanted more information about us. We sent her emails about ourselves and what our family life had been like growing up.

After a few weeks, while I was working at the daycare, I received the dreaded email telling me how sorry the mom-to-be was. She had told the birth father what she wanted to do, but he was not willing to relinquish his rights. Since for any legal adoption both parents have to be willing to sign off their rights, this put an abrupt end to my dream. I was devastated.

March 2011

By now I had finished reading my book series about God. I felt close to Him, closer than I ever had. So I kept talking to God and asking Him why. What was the purpose for this pain? I knew there had to be a reason, that God had a purpose, and I trusted Him.

Two weeks to the day from our finding out that the birth father didn't want to give up his rights, we had another proposition. It was from the same doctor who had found the birth mother for us.

This time the doctor knew of a nurse, Abigail, with whom she had previously worked. Abigail was the grandmother of three children. The kids were nine years old, seven years old, and five years old. Abigail had adopted them, and the children had been living with her for almost a year. Now, however, she had developed pulmonary fibrosis and was no longer able to care for them.

She wanted them to be adopted out together and not be placed back into foster care. Abigail and the kids were originally from the Osceola area but were currently living in Rock Port, Missouri. Abigail frequently went back to Osceola, as did Scott and I, to visit family. How ironic!

CHAPTER 4

The Meeting

April 2011

After quite a few weeks of phone tag with Abigail, given our mutually busy schedules, we finally met up with her and her boyfriend, Pete, at a bar and grill.

Abigail and Pete were very friendly and ordered a round of beer for all. Scott declined and ordered a Pepsi. I was a little taken aback by the round of beer. I thought this was more of a formal meeting, and it was only noon. *Oh well*, I thought. *It's Saturday—let's kick back.*

Abigail showed us pictures of the children and identified them by name: Erica, Kayla, and Ethan. They seemed excited about the prospect of our adopting the kids.

"Stacy is bad news," Abigail had announced of her daughter. "All the counseling they have gone through says it would not be good for the kids to see her. Stacy knows we are adopting them out and agrees that this is in the best interest of the kids. She knows she can't take care of them."

Abigail ordered another round for herself and Pete. "Now, you know that there is no state aid for raising the kids," Abigail put in. "That means there is no supplemental income like you would get in foster care, and no Medicaid from Iowa."

Abigail made a point of bringing this up a couple of different times. We understood. We didn't want to do this for the money. We wanted a family!

May 13, 2011

A few weeks later we met with the kids for the first time at Abigail's house in Missouri. Ethan, five, was a social butterfly. He talked our ears off about himself and showed us lots of pictures he had drawn. He liked baseball, dogs, and drawing. Ethan has dark blonde hair with brown eyes that light up when he smiles.

Kayla, seven, gave us little attention besides an occasional grunt. She was more interested in what was in the refrigerator to eat. She had long, unkempt, dirty blonde hair with bright blue eyes. We noticed that she was very flexible as she dropped down on the floor into the splits to watch TV. She enjoyed gymnastics, soccer, and the color pink, we learned.

Erica, nine, didn't say a word to us. We learned from Abigail that Erica enjoyed playing school. She wanted to be a teacher and was very organized. Erica also had long, dark blonde hair with the same dark brown eyes as Ethan. Her face was more serious, and she seemed to be hiding something.

As we left that day, Erica rode her scooter in the driveway in a circle, glaring at us. She never said a word. I realized then that it was going to be hard breaking down her walls and getting her to trust me. I was excited and scared at the same time.

Journal Entry

This is it. I know that God wouldn't lead me astray. This is what I was meant to do. I am supposed to save these kids. I can give them love, a stable home, and structure, and they will flourish and become successful adults! I went to school and received a degree in child development. I figure I have a good idea of how kids operate. Granted, I have more experience with younger kids, but I have worked in day care centers all of these years.

I was taught in college about nature vs. nurture and the continuing dialogue about which is stronger. I believe nurture is stronger. Situations influence a person. If you get kids out of bad situations they can flourish—they just need the opportunity to do so.

CHAPTER 5

A Glimpse into Reality

May 21, 2011

We went for another visit with the kids a week later, bringing Harley along this time. Erica still didn't say much, but she did warm up to Harley. She sat on the floor and petted him while he sat beside her. Harley was very patient with her as I watched in wonder. It was almost as though Harley knew she might become part of his family.

Abigail announced that she needed to do a Shopko run. Erica wanted to join her, and before long so did Ethan. Soon an argument broke out about who was going to get to go along. I watched the spectacle unfold as Ethan jumped up and down, using a high, whiney voice that made me recoil as though I were hearing fingernails scraping against a chalkboard. Abigail gave in to him right away.

"That's not fair—I said I wanted to go first!" Erica shouted.

"You guys are supposed to be visiting with Heather and Scott," Abigail protested.

"It's okay," I assured her. "May I come along too? Then they can spend time with both of us."

Erica shot me a look.

I felt bad for her. I know what it is like being the oldest and always having to share everything with younger siblings.

Scott decided to stay back with Kayla and Pete, and we left on our shopping excursion. It was raining outside, so Abigail grabbed an oversized umbrella on our way out the door.

Once we got to Shopko there was an argument about who was going to push the cart. Ethan could barely see over the top, but he got to push it first, after resorting to his whiney voice again. After he had rammed the cart into various things, Abigail finally took that chore away from him and gave it to Erica.

Ethan threw himself onto the floor in a full-blown temper tantrum, like a two year old. I stood there in amazement as he kicked and screamed. I had gone to school for a degree in child development a few years back. My schooling told me to walk away from him, but Abigail handed him the oversized umbrella we had used to take refuge from the rain. This small gesture calmed Ethan down. He carried it as we made our way around the store.

Abigail told Scott and me that we were free to start disciplining the children as we saw fit. "Especially if you see me struggling. It's getting harder to keep up with them."

As we continued to walk around Shopko, Erica got tired of pushing the cart. She and Ethan started walking behind Abigail, and I followed them. Ethan opened the umbrella and hit Erica with it.

"ETHAN, KNOCK IT OFF!" Erica shouted at him.

He opened and closed it repeatedly, hitting things with it as we walked. My heart rate increased as I observed his defiance, Abigail looking distraught. My daycare expertise kicked in.

I put my hands on Ethan's shoulders to stop him from walking and whispered into his ear, "Ethan, I'm giving you one warning. Keep the umbrella closed or you are going to lose it."

I let go of his shoulders and we started walking again. He lasted ten seconds before looking back at me, opening the umbrella, and hitting Erica.

"ETHAN!" she screeched.

This set off an anxious feeling in my stomach. I immediately felt bad for Erica, having her shopping experience with her grandma ruined by an annoying little brother.

I went to Ethan and took the umbrella. He once again threw himself onto the floor, and I walked away. Abigail was far ahead of us. I noticed her turn around once, but she saw the performance that was unfolding and kept moving, as though she didn't know who we were.

By the sound of Ethan's wails I could tell when he got off the floor and started coming back toward me. I closed the umbrella and wondered how many times he acted like this to get his way. I knew people were watching, but I really didn't care.

Ethan came from behind and started hitting me in my lower back.

"GIVE IT TO ME! IT'S MINE! GIVE IT TO ME!" He tried to grab the umbrella out of my hands while he yelled.

It was embarrassing holding the umbrella over my head while he screamed at me and tried to crawl up my body. I tried my best to ignore Ethan's behavior. I finally got the idea that maybe he wouldn't do this to his grandma.

I found Abigail, handed her the umbrella, and told her what had happened, counseling her not to give it back to him. Ethan calmed down a little with her. He didn't try hitting her or climbing up her body. However, he still used his whiney voice and continued the cries of protest: "IT'S MINE. GIVE IT TO ME!"

This lasted for a couple more minutes before Abigail gave in and handed him the umbrella. I heard her tell him, "DO NOT OPEN IT."

Instantly, Ethan stopped crying and turned around and looked at me. His eyes glinted evilly. He had gotten his way. His glare gave me the chills. It was going to take a lot of work to get him to stop having temper tantrums whenever he didn't gain the upper hand. Consistency and love, I assured myself, would do it.

CHAPTER 6

A Little More Insight

June 2011

Over the next few weeks we met with a lawyer. Abigail and the kids lived in a different state, so we had to abide by interstate laws. We needed to become foster parents for a year before we could adopt them. We also had to complete a home study with an adoption agency.

Abigail's pulmonary fibrosis condition had worsened. She didn't want to wait a year. She wanted to speed the process up. I was fine with that! Happy, actually!

Abigail had a friend who lived just on the other side of the state line in Nebraska. Abigail changed her address to her friend's and picked up her mail there. That made her a legal resident of Nebraska. We no longer had to follow interstate adoption law. I felt bad that we were lying but was excited that the adoption would happen faster; I knew this had to be God's doing.

Over the summer we visited the kids every weekend. We went to parks and movies together and enjoyed each other's company. I started seeing Ethan gain better control of his body and start to listen to Scott and me when redirected. I also saw the girls warming up to us. I felt as though this could work out and foresaw our becoming an instantly cohesive family.

Scott, Pete, Abigail, and I met with the girls' counselors and had a discussion with them. Ethan hadn't begun seeing a counselor yet. Abigail felt that he was too little and probably didn't remember much of his early years.

We learned a little more about the girls from the counselors. They were excited and happy for the girls to be getting a family with a mom and a dad. The counselors discouraged us from maintaining a connection with Stacy.

"She is detrimental to their well-being. The longer you can keep her out of their lives the better," they explained.

August 2011

While the kids were on a vacation with their extended family I visited them for a day. Scott decided not to go and worked instead. The family went to a cabin on a lake. I sat in a lawn chair under a shelter house with the kids' aunt and enjoyed a couple of beverages with her. As we visited, we enjoyed the warm day and watched the kids play on a giant jumping pad in the middle of the lake. We could hear their shrieks of excitement in the water. The kids loved water. It seemed to be their happy place, the domain in which all was well. They invented little games and actually played together.

"Can you give me any more info on their past and what their trauma was?" I asked their aunt.

"Sure," she replied. "Stacy was a good mom at one time. She used to keep the kids clean and fed and enforced good manners. Once she met Trinity, her current wife, Stacy got into drugs and all sorts of bad situations. She left the kids with whomever and ran around. There were times when she wouldn't come back for days, and the kids had no idea who was going to be taking care of them."

"That's awful," I acknowledged.

The kids' aunt fidgeted from side to side in her chair as she continued.

"The kids' dad, Chad, is lazy and an alcoholic. He tried to have the kids live with him but couldn't handle the stress of young children, working, and finances. Once he found out there was no state aid for him to raise his OWN kids, he didn't want to be responsible for them," she finished.

The aunt got up to make another drink. As she poured her drink into her glass she continued, "The kids have been in multiple foster homes, and they were removed abruptly from one of them."

"Oh, why is that?" I asked.

"Well, there may have been sexual assault to Kayla there, but the suspicion was never verified."

"OH, THE POOR THING!" I exclaimed.

"Yeah, but it wasn't confirmed," the aunt repeated. She finished pouring her drink and sat back down. "That's when my mom, Abigail, wanted to adopt them and get them out of DHS and foster homes. My first cousin, Marie, stepped up with her husband, Kenneth, and they took the kids for eight months while Abigail got the legal work done."

"How did the kids do with your cousin?" I asked.

"They did great," the aunt replied. "They provided a stable home and the kids seemed happy. The kids really liked Marie's son, Collin, especially Ethan. Collin would take Ethan hunting and fishing."

The aunt changed the subject, offering, "Let me tell you about the kids. Ethan has a lot of personality, but he lacks in respect and listening. He loves fishing and being outside. Erica has a huge heart. She's the ringleader of the group and acts like her siblings' mother. Poor thing pretty much raised Ethan and Kayla. Erica can be very anxious and scared of change," the aunt informed me. "Kayla likes the color pink, and her favorite stuffed animal is her pig."

As she started to tell me about Kayla, I could tell that their aunt was troubled.

"Kayla reminds me of Stacy. The way she acts, the looks she gives, and the way she talks. Stacy and I don't get along. She's not a nice person. Kayla reminds me so much of Stacy that I almost resent Kayla," the aunt admitted. "I am very aware that it is not Kayla's fault and that Kayla is a separate individual from Stacy. However, I just can't help noticing that Kayla is a spitting image of her."

The aunt reiterated what Abigail had said: "The counselors said it would be detrimental for Stacy to be in their lives. It would be best for the kids to keep seeing counselors in Omaha so they can keep working on their feelings of abandonment and work through the trauma."

"I understand. We'll definitely get that lined up," I reassured her.

As the day went on the kids became rambunctious. They were mouthy and rude to each other and to the adults. This was opposite behavior from what we had seen when Scott and I were with them. When it was time for me to leave, they didn't want to give hugs goodbye and seemed out of sorts. Maybe they didn't like saying goodbye . . .

When I got into my vehicle and was driving away, I cried. *Maybe we can't do this. They have a lot of baggage. I don't know if I can handle all of this, and the way they treat each other and adults is not how I was raised. It's not too late—we can still back out.*

I called Scott and shared with him my concerns.

"We can do this—we are not giving up. It'll get better once they move in with us. Remember how we wanted more out of life and not be stuck in a rut?" Scott calmly replied.

"Okay, you're right," I conceded.

CHAPTER 7

Our House

August 2011

In 2008 the housing market had crashed. We had our townhouse that was only in my name, and we were completely upside down with it financially. It had only two bedrooms. We could convert a third room into a bedroom if needed, but it was a really small space.

My friend at church had a neighbor who was looking for renters for her house. Her grown children had lived there but were now moving out. The house was in a neighborhood I had always wanted to live in, right by the local school! The woman who owned the house heard our story, and, being as we were unable to purchase outright, we made an agreement to receive the house on a contract for deed. Yay, God!

We chose to walk away from the townhouse, in the process destroying my good credit. This is something I am not proud of; still, it took a giant leap of faith. I really had no idea what was going to happen but knew I had to do what was best for the kids.

On one of the final visits to our townhouse, the kids sat outside while I took a picture of them. Harley wanted in the picture and sat in front of the kids. He was proud of his children. They all look very happy with smiling faces—including Harley! I believe this was a true sign from God that things were going exactly the way they needed to go. I still to this day have that picture in a frame that I keep close.

CHAPTER 8

The First Move

September 2011

We went to Abigail's house to pick up the kids with a U-Haul a few days before school started. They were all a chatter as we boxed up their belongings and moved furniture into the moving truck.

As we got ready to leave Abigail's house we decided to take a picture. While Ethan hung in the tree, Erica and Kayla stood underneath it.

I heard Erica tell her siblings sternly but quietly, "DON'T SMILE."

Moments later Abigail pleaded with them to smile. Erica was definitely the ringleader the other two would follow to the end. I supposed this was a hard day for them. I was ecstatic to start this new adventure, but they were probably terrified.

We drove the two hours back to Omaha. They each talked about their bedrooms they had painted a few weeks earlier with us, and how each of them was going to arrange their room. They were excited about the big backyard and being able to walk to a park just down the street.

When we got there we had lots of help from neighbors as we unloaded the moving van. Our church family came to help too. Once the van was unloaded and things placed in the appropriate rooms, our extra help dispersed. Soon it was Scott, Abigail, the kids, and me. We helped the children arrange their rooms and get settled in. Abigail decided to spend the night to help ease the first night fears.

Ethan and Kayla had no problems going to their rooms to wind down. I read a story to Ethan and got him tucked in. He was mostly unpacked but had a few things left to do. He had the bathroom right across from his room so he wouldn't have to go far in case of an emergency.

I went to tuck Kayla in.

Her room was unpacked, but nothing had been put away. Kayla would find a home for something and then rehome it within a few minutes. She asked me for a nightlight, as she was scared of the dark, and pleaded for me to leave her bedroom door open. We strategically placed her in the room closest to our bedroom so she could see our door and feel safe. This sleeping behavior in a seven-year-old concerned me.

I went downstairs to Erica's room. She enjoyed having her bedroom downstairs, where it was a little cooler. We were blessed to have found this house. It had enough bedrooms for everyone and was structured the way the kids needed it.

Erica was sitting on her bed reading. She didn't look up when I came into her room to say goodnight. Everything in her room was put away, including knickknacks displayed neatly on her shelves. She is definitely organized.

I went to bed both excited and full of anxiety. I was uncertain where the anxiety was coming from, but it was hard to sleep with my stomach full of butterflies. Still, I felt certain this would pass.

CHAPTER 9

Adjusting

October 2011

The first few weeks were great. Scott and I decided I could quit my job, and I started the process of opening my own daycare so I could be home with the kids every day.

School started, and everyone seemed to adjust to a new home life. We got into a new routine.

We enrolled the kids in counseling and brought them to our church on a regular basis. The children had not gone to church much before. They were new to God. Our church got them each a Bible, and we started talking about God. I read to Ethan out of his preschool Bible every night and enjoyed refreshing myself with the stories.

Some weekends we went back to the Osceola area. We visited Scott's family and did all the things we were used to: camping, canoeing, or snowmobiling in the winter.

Abigail started out calling nightly when the kids first moved in but downgraded this into weekly calls. Every other weekend the kids stayed with her. The kids' favorite joint activity was to play school. Erica was always the teacher and Kayla and Ethan her students. They had homework assignments and conducted writing and math classes.

Sometimes I heard them arguing in their basement play area. Kayla and Ethan would get tired of Erica bossing them around and would break off and create their own classroom.

I think playing school was Erica's way of keeping control over her siblings so that she could mother them. Her primary area of stability was at school; that was the setting in which she felt safest and knew in turn how to keep her siblings safe.

Erica and I did not hit it off right away. She was the mother figure to her siblings, so to have some stranger come in and act like a mom was different for all of them. Ethan and Kayla looked to Erica for guidance with every decision they made. It was difficult for Erica to let go of control over her siblings because in her eyes, and theirs, Erica was the mom.

When I asked Kayla one day to take out the garbage, she looked at Erica for confirmation as to whether she should do so.

"Why are we expected to do chores?" Erica asked, after returning Kayla's glance.

"It's part of helping out and being a family," I explained.

"Are we going to get paid for it?" Erica pursued. "Grandma used to pay us for doing chores. I think we need to get paid for it."

"All right," Scott chimed in. "We'll make a chore chart for all of you, and you can get paid for each chore."

"Okay, Kayla, take out the garbage," Erica instructed.

I don't believe in this. I would rather instill the value of helping out because we are family. Maybe as time went by we could do away with the chore chart and with treating our children as employees. I believe in nurturing. We could get there.

As time went on, the kids began to open up to us more and more. They shared stories about their mom's friends and experiences.

Ethan told us about a time when his mom had a friend come over who wore an orange jumpsuit. The jumpsuit had writing on the back, and Ethan claimed that he'd had to go to his room while they visited.

Erica told a story about one of the houses they had lived in that had tarp hanging inside it. It had a real funny smell that she didn't like. She reported that they had been living with Stacy and Trinity at the time.

Ethan and Erica both reminisced about a time when Ethan didn't have a bed and slept on a child's foldout chair. Ethan would get up and go lie with Erica because he was cold and didn't have a blanket.

After our conversation I stared in wonder yet again as I felt the anxiety rise in the pit of my stomach. What kinds of people had they been having at their house? The kids got up in the middle of the night and took food to their rooms. I found hidden food regularly in their bedrooms. Scott grew very frustrated with this.

"There is plenty to eat. They shouldn't take food to their rooms. It belongs in the kitchen," he would complain.

Ethan told me one time while we were working on homework together, "We didn't have food to eat, but Erica would find us stuff. I would sit on the floor and eat pop tarts. They are my favorite! When we ran out of pop tarts Erica would find us other food, like oatmeal and noodles, and we would eat right out of the box."

I brought up that conversation to Scott and the kids' counselors. There were a few other issues we worked on intently with the counselors.

We kept working together with Erica's counselor on the concept of what a great job she had done with Ethan and Kayla, though now it was time for her to be a kid, too.

We were working with Ethan on how to follow directions and be in control of his body. His first response was to argue and throw temper tantrums, as in the incident in Shopko.

Kayla loved to help out around the house and to please people. She would organize anything but her own room and belongings. That included the kitchen and bathroom cupboards, making it hard to find things when we wanted them. There were a few disturbing physical actions we were also working through in counseling. I could tell that she was troubled, but she probably didn't even know what was bothering her.

Kayla made inappropriate gestures with her pelvis. She was able to do a twerking motion and get air to go in and out of her body to sound like farting noises. When she did this Erica and Ethan would watch and laugh hysterically at her, which made her want to do it all the more.

Erica and Kayla also liked to pretend they were "making out." When I caught them doing this, I always cut it short. I'm not sure whether or not this was an attention-seeking device.

Finally, we were working on a situation that was happening between Kayla and Ethan. They would be playing in the living room and get into wrestling matches. Sometimes I would find them humping each other. They should not have known anything about humping at the ages of six and eight.

CHAPTER 10

Celebration

May 2012

Our adoption was finalized in May of 2012. We had opted for a private adoption and needed only a lawyer and a judge. The judge was from our congregation and was excited to be a part of our new family union. We ended up opting out of taking classes through an adoption agency or having DHS involved, finding these choices to facilitate the process.

As part of the adoption agreement, Abigail intended to apply her social security benefits to the kids in the event of her death. Beginning immediately, we would on a monthly basis receive a stipend for each child to help aid in raising them.

"I want to make sure the kids are taken care of. I want them to have the chance to go to college," Abigail had told us. "This will help you, being there will be no state aid for you. In the event of my death, the money will triple."

"Triple?" Scott had asked, surprised.

"It's not about the money," I assured her.

We signed papers, knowing that the agreement was to extend the kids' birth family affiliation. We chose an open adoption so that they could still see their grandma, aunts, uncles, and cousins.

We signed an agreement with Abigail that we would allow her to have the children visit her one weekend a month as long as this was in the best interest of the kids. We wanted to keep as much stability in their lives as we could.

June 2012

We had a giant party at our house in celebration of our adoption being finalized. We rented tents and tables and chairs. We invited all of our church family, our friends from Iowa, and all of our extended family.

Scott's mom and older brother, Kyle, came the day before to help with setup. Kyle's wife, Megan, and their children, Kelly and Ryker, were a huge help.

"Ryker and I can entertain the kids while you meal prep," Kelly suggested.

"That'd be great!" I exclaimed.

Kelly was just a few years older than the girls, and they got along well. Ryker is a year older than Erica. Ethan and Ryker were inseparable when they were together. They enjoyed playing Legos and video games.

It was nice that our families welcomed the kids into their lives as though they had been ours all along.

Scott's younger brother, Russell, also has two daughters, Jenny and Becky. Becky and Kelly are the same age, and Jenny is a few years older.

My parents, sister, and brother also attended our celebration, in addition to which we invited Abigail and the children's aunts, along with Kenneth and Marie and their son, Collin.

Collin had moved back in with his parents to help with the kids while waiting for Abigail's adoption to take place. This family holds a very special place in the kids' eyes, comprising the first stable home they had known. The kids were so happy to see all of them. Especially Collin.

Marie, who loves to take pictures, arranged them for a photo shoot on the deck. They posed in funny positions and smiled! I think the kids see these family members as another set of grandparents, not as cousins.

CHAPTER 11

The Truth

August 2012

The kids continued to visit Abigail about once a month for a while. When they came back home, though, they would be out of sorts—very anxious, rude, mouthy, and disrespectful. It would take about a day and a half to get them back into routine and untriggered. They always seemed agitated upon their return, but they still wanted to see her and claimed that the visits were going well.

Eventually we found out that Abigail had been lying to us. We discovered that during this entire time she had been receiving money from Iowa, the state from which she had originally adopted the children, even though we had adopted them from her. No wonder she had kept reiterating that there would be no state aid!

After the state of Iowa had busted her, she apologized and had to repay to us the money she had received during that time. We had never intended to receive any money for the kids. That hadn't been part of the deal, but we were able to apply the funds to our adoption debt and found them to be an unanticipated blessing.

At around the same time Abigail started telling us that the kids should be seeing their birth mom, Stacy, again. We were shocked, as in the beginning she had been adamant that they should not see her at all. Abigail had heard from the counselors, as we had, that exposure to Stacy would be detrimental to their health.

Abigail told the kids that their mom and dad had lost their parental rights to DHS and were taken away. We were confused now and didn't know what to believe. We decided to ask Kenneth and Marie when we were on a short visit with them at their house what they knew about the kids' history.

"OH, A LOT!" Marie exclaimed. "I have paperwork, so let me find it. I'll make copies so you can have it."

"Every time the kids would visit us when they lived with Abigail, they would leave an article of their belongings here purposely. They would leave things under beds or hidden in closets. I really believe this was so that the kids felt they could have an excuse to come back to get their things," Marie told us before we left.

Their home had truly been the kids' only stable environment before our own home.

Marie gave us paperwork to keep that had come from the Department of Human Services and the social workers who had worked with the family through foster care and the adoption process to Abigail.

Later that night, when I was alone, I unfolded the paperwork and read:

"Reasons for removal from Parental Home.

Initially it was due to Mom, Stacy, leaving the children with whomever while she was running around. Dad signed a safety plan agreeing not to allow mom unsupervised contact. He then permitted unsupervised contact and the children were removed. Dad, Chad, eventually had the children returned to him and did well for a period of time. He eventually reported he can no longer manage the stress of three young children, working, finances, etc., and he wanted the children to return to their mother. The children were placed with mom, who it was thought was doing well enough to keep the children safe. Eventually mom contacted DHS and self-reported that she was using meth again.

The children were removed and placed with relatives. Dad voluntarily signed his rights off. Mom did as well, but her attorney did not submit the paperwork, allowing her time to think about it. Mom changed her mind and stated she wanted to work towards reunification. Mom stated this but did not follow through with mental health and substance abuse treatment. Eventually both parents voluntarily signed off their parental rights. An approved home study has been completed for Abigail, grandmother, for foster home licensing.

The children were bonded with their parents. The parents appeared to have done some appropriate parenting. The children were kept clean, were well fed, and had good manners. Mom Stacy was allegedly sexually abused by her older brother for several years when she was a child. She was involved in juvenile court as a juvenile and reports having had something like twenty placements. She has also reportedly been diagnosed with borderline personality disorder and possible bipolar. She has taken medication sporadically for depression but has not consistently followed through with mental health care even though she has been court committed to do so. Mom has abused alcohol and has tested positive for meth. She has self-reported suicide attempts. Mom also recently reported an overdose of cocaine and ecstasy; this has not been verified, as it occurred out of state. Mom has been involved with both men and women in intimate relationships.

Mom has a substantiated report for dependent adult abuse. When married to her children's father, Chad, she was working at a residential care facility. She took one of the residents from the facility to a hotel in Des Moines and was using drugs with him.

Chad, father, has a mother who is mentally ill, and he self-reports that he and his siblings had to take care of one another. His parents were divorced and his father later died, which troubled him greatly. It is suspected that Chad may suffer from some anxiety related issue, and he was encouraged to seek mental health care but declined to do so. He also abused alcohol (although he doesn't see it that way). There was one incident in which he was taken from his home by ambulance to the hospital because of a very high blood alcohol count.

Stacy and Chad have continued to have an enmeshed relationship; they admit having physical relations even after they were split up and had moved on to other partners. They are now divorced but hang around together on occasion. Both parents will alternatively be supportive of one another and then tell on the other parent when it suits their needs. Both of these parents have observed inappropriate relationships with their own parents. Both Stacy and Chad's parents were divorced but continued to have a relationship with the ex-spouse. Stacy's mother, Abigail, was sexually abused by her own brother and is receiving counseling for that. Abigail has a very conflictual relationship with her daughter; Stacy has consistently stated that she hates her mother.

The children were initially placed with foster parents when removed the first time. They were subsequently moved due to concerns with the foster home. They were then placed with a couple, where they remained until return to the custody of their father. The children resided with their father for a number of months, and then he eventually reported he was struggling to care for them. He was working full-time, going through a bankruptcy, in the process of divorcing Stacy, losing his home, etc. It is also believed he may have been struggling with anxiety and depression, but he was unwilling to seek out assistance for those issues.

Stacy gave the appearance of being stable. She reported to have a strong support and had an appropriate home. It was believed she had not used drugs in a number of months. The children were returned to Stacy. After several months she self-reported that she was again using meth. There was some question about whether she really was or whether this was a ruse to have the children removed from her care so she can again have less responsibilities. In any event the children were placed with the paternal great aunt and uncle. Within a couple of days of being placed there Stacy was creating conflict with the placement and they asked that the children be removed.

Stacy's mom, Abigail, then came forth and wanted the children placed with her. She volunteered to come to Iowa and stay in the family home so the children wouldn't be displaced from their home/school setting. Abigail is employed in Rock Port, and when things weren't quickly resolved she needed to return to Missouri.

Chad agreed to have the children return to him but did not follow through. The children were briefly in Missouri with Abigail for a visit but had to return due to interstate compact regulations. They were then placed with Stacy's cousin and spouse, Kenneth and Marie, where they have remained since that time.

Kenneth and Marie are a couple with grown children, and they both work out of the home. Kenneth and Marie have provided a stable, supportive home, and the children have all responded well to their structure. Kenneth and Marie both work while the kids attend school. The children have a regular meal time, bed/bath, etc. They frequently go to their Grandma

Abigail's on weekends. They had been having supervised visits with their mother prior but these visits were not consistent.

Services were offered to both parents for a final visit, and they declined. They likely believe that because the children will be placed with Stacy's mother that contact will continue and they didn't need to participate in a final visit."

After reading all of this, I wanted to cry. I had no idea what we had gotten ourselves into. Abigail had never shared this information with us. I did not know about the mental health issues and felt betrayed about the manner in which we were getting into the middle of this. I shared the information with Scott. At this point we lost all trust in Abigail.

CHAPTER 12

Stacy

September 2012

A few weeks later we received a letter from Stacy. I don't know how she got our address, as we had moved and were in a contract for deed. I could take a pretty good guess, though . . .

"Scott and Heather,

I don't know what you guys have been told but I can probably tell you it was all a lie. My three babies you have right now were never supposed to go anywhere outside the family. Before the rights were signed off, I sat down and talked to my mom on what I want to happen.

The only reason I signed off was because my mom asked me to, to get DHS out of our lives. After all was said and done she was going to sign back over rights to Chad and me. I was still able to take kids whenever, but only under the condition I wasn't using drugs.

I never thought in a million years my kids would be taken out of the family and to someone else. As you probably know or heard my mom and I have never liked each other, and she used my kids as leverage to get back at me. Before you got the kids she also told Chad he could have custody of them.

I really want my kids back as much as Chad and hope for that day to come so they can say who they want to live with. I want you to think about having your own kids and all of a sudden not being able to see or talk to them.

I don't understand why I can't talk to them. It's not like they're going to forget their mom and dad. All I'm asking is to say hi. It's almost been a year and it's not fair to me or my kids. I don't want them to think I gave up or don't want a part in their life because I do. Please take time to have them make me a picture and for you to call me."

I responded back with my own letter:

"Dear Stacy,

Your mom has told us about the pretense of wanting to keep the children in the family. When she adopted them she was going to give them back to Chad under the understanding that he would provide for them and be sober. However, Chad did not uphold his end, stopped wanting to see the children, and didn't stay sober. Your mom continues to get ill and knew that neither of you were capable of taking back the children.

You say you were able to take the kids whenever if you were not using drugs. The last I heard you are. You said that you only signed off to get DHS out of your lives. Why did DHS get involved to begin with? DHS was there to protect your children and be their advocate. DHS were the ones thinking about what was best for the kids, being you and Chad were incapable of doing that.

I'm sorry that your mom and you don't get along. I do believe that she used the kids as leverage against you. I think she used the children for a lot of things, including money.

Scott and I are now in the kids' life and always thinking what is best for them. Honestly, we are the first ones in their lives to do that besides Kenneth and Marie. We are happy to be in the children's lives now and thrilled that we can end your family's game of using the children as pawns.

I do think about having my own kids—these three are my own. If I had given birth to them I would have never made bad enough choices to have DHS involved in the first place. I would have worked with DHS to keep my children instead of playing the system like you and your mom do.

There is a reason why you can't see or speak to them— you fill them with lies and deceit. You are never sober or clean from drugs around them. When we talk to counselors and other professionals about you, they all say the same thing— "It would be detrimental to the children to see or speak to her."

We never speak ill of you to the kids. We do tell them that you love them very much because I know you do. However, in the best interest of the kids, due to how much they have seen and been through, it is unwise of us to let the kids see you.

When they graduate high school they are adults, and then therefore can make their own decision of what is best for themselves."

I felt so much better once I had put the pen down. I took both letters, carefully folded them within each other and placed them back into the original envelope. I then took the envelope and placed it into the safe. I wrote my response with no intention of ever sending it to Stacy. I just needed to say what I needed to say.

CHAPTER 13

Hodgepodge of Stressers

November 2012

We allowed the children to continue to see Abigail because we didn't have the heart to completely separate them from their birth family. Abigail's health was failing quickly, so we stayed with the kids on their visits instead of leaving them there alone. That worked better for all, as we no longer trusted Abigail and she could no longer keep up with them.

On November 20, 2012, all three kids were baptized in Christ! The kids' aunts and Abigail were there, along with Scott's and my families. The kids each had two baptismal sponsors, who ended up being aunts and uncles from the different sides of our families. They each had their own specially made cake that represented something they loved: Erica cats, Ethan baseball, and Kayla soccer. I could see the love for the kids radiating from all around.

December 2012

We barely survived the holidays. Scott had his rules that needed to be followed. Among them: when we traveled the car needed to be in park before we could take off our seatbelts, socks were to be worn in the house during the winter, and we needed to be sure we were all eating healthily.

The seat belt rule would normally have been a good one for most families. Except that Scott would actually sit there for a moment before putting the car into park to see whether anyone prematurely unbuckled their seatbelt. If he heard one click it had to be strapped back on. He even caught me unlocking my seat belt a couple times before he had fully moved the gearshift into park.

Mealtimes were always stressful for Ethan. The kids needed to eat at mealtimes and hence not be snacking too much between meals. Expected mealtime etiquette included sitting up straight, using silverware correctly, and absolutely never singing at the table. The kids needed to have a protein and a healthy portion size.

At seven years old by this time, Ethan had the most trouble with this. He still hadn't mastered how to appropriately use his silverware. I worked with him on this, but for some reason he couldn't let his spoon touch his mouth. So when he ate soup or cereal it turned out to be a really loud, slurping mess. Sometimes I questioned whether he was doing this on purpose or whether he really had a problem letting the spoon touch his mouth.

We did enjoy a family getaway over Christmas break. Scott is quieter about his rules once we get around other people. We went with Scott's family to a cabin and enjoyed snowmobiling. The kids had a great time with the cousins, Ryker, Kelly, Jenny, and Becky. They were bonding together, and it was great!

January 2013

I woke up with stomach problems. For several months afterward I couldn't eat without getting sick. I had severe stomach pains and intestinal discomfort. Luckily, working at home with daycare I had the option of making whatever food I could handle. I had every scan and test the doctors could possibly think of. I lost a lot of weight and was starting to feel miserable and down.

Summer 2013

We went on our first family vacation. We traveled to South Dakota and saw Mount Rushmore, camping along the way. Russell, Becky, and Jenny joined us. It was fun, but stressful. Scott was out of sorts being we were traveling. Don't forget the seatbelt and food rules! I tried to maintain as much routine as possible, but everyone still seemed on edge. Maybe it was more of a regular family vacation. Does anyone's vacation run smoothly?

Abigail called while we were on our way out to South Dakota. She had received news that a lung had come in for her, and she was going in immediately for her lung transplant surgery. That was big news! Good news and bad news, actually, all depending on how the surgery would go. If well, she could enjoy a productive new phase of life. If badly, she might not make it out of the operation.

I quietly shared the news with Scott. Of course I prayed, but I didn't see fit under the circumstances to tell the kids about the procedure. We opted to share the news after the fact so they wouldn't have to grapple with adult fears.

The operation went well, and Abigail received a new lung! God is good!

Journal Entry: September 11, 2013

I had my appointment with a dietician today. If it doesn't come from the ground or basically God, then don't eat it! How fitting!

I also saw an intestinal specialist. Nine months later, a whole ton of tests, and they still don't know why I can't eat and feel sick. He asked me today, "Could this be psychosomatic?"

Really?! How could this be in my head? He suggested that I look into reducing my stress. Now how am I going to do that? I can't get rid of my family!

CHAPTER 14

Back to Helpless

October 15, 2013

Kayla woke up late again and was clearly nursing a grudge. As I tried to care for the daycare kids who had already arrived, she stormed around like an angry tornado, leaving a destructive wake everywhere she went. Kayla slammed everything she touched (think cupboard doors), did a lot of heavy sighing, and gave off this aura of anger.

This caused me a lot of anxiety. I couldn't concentrate. I felt as though I were out of control myself, and this gave me that anxious butterfly feeling in my stomach. I had long since recognized a need in myself to want to keep the kids happy. They should, I reasoned, always be happy; after all, look what we had done for them. I tried to keep my anxiety under control with deep breaths as I cared for the daycare kids and did my best to remain calm.

The final straw for Kayla was discovering that there was no hot meal to take to school. That meant that she would have to take a sandwich, which she hated. She couldn't find anything else to pack for an entrée.

"Pack the meat and bread separately, being you don't like them together," I suggested.

Remember that healthy meals were one of the rules that Scott liked to enforce. Kayla didn't like the school lunch selection and wanted only to bring food from home, so every day she packed a lunch. I was trying very hard to keep up with the school lunch rules Scott insisted the children follow: an entrée that had protein, a fruit, and a vegetable.

I checked her lunch. She had one small piece of sandwich meat, one slice of bread, one apple, and a big Tupperware container of crackers.

"Kayla, you can't take the crackers and fill up on them because they are junk food. You need to bring more meat," I pointed out to her.

She immediately stormed over to the kitchen garbage and threw her lunch away.

"Why did you make me get rid of my lunch? Nothing I do is ever good enough!"

At that she stormed out of the house without saying goodbye.

I should have applauded her on what a fine job she had done on her lunch. It was in fact a good lunch. But this was one of Scott's rules I needed to follow. I worked hard to enforce Scott's rules. After all, I rationalized, a husband and wife are a team, and the wife should submit to the husband.

After the other kids had left for school, I changed daycare diapers in the bathroom and contemplated why these kids continuously blamed others for their actions. The children chose to be angry as their go-to emotional response. They had a way of taking what I said and twisting it. Still, I knew that God has brought us all together for a purpose and that Scott and I were here with them to help.

Journal Entry

How long do you keep loving others who do not love you, who resent you? How long do you turn the other cheek? Some days I feel this adoption eating at my soul and my marriage. I know I need to keep on. This is the path God has chosen for me. He knows that I will do it because He will be with me the whole time. What God leads you into, He will lead you through.

Help me, Lord, to keep my patience and my faith front and center. Help me to stay focused on you, especially when the devil is right in my face. I know you will not forsake me. Help me, Lord, to listen to you and lead these children where you intend. And if someday there is no hope anymore for someone, help me to let go. Help, Lord—only you know the outcome of our lives.

CHAPTER 15

Scott

October 19, 2013

I discovered that we had no money. Granted, we had *some* money, but when medical bills were not getting paid I really questioned Scott where our money was going.

"I don't understand what is happening to our money . . . ," I announced to him. I was starting to get gutsier talking to him and not letting him intimidate me.

"I am making good money with my daycare, and there should be no reason for bills not to get paid," I continued.

I could tell by the look on his face that he was getting upset. He still startled me, but I was gaining more respect for myself.

"I would like to take over the checkbook," I finished.

"Fine. Being you are a perfect bitch and can do better, you should just do it yourself."

Excellent. I would.

November 13, 2013

Last night Scott was in a bad mood after taking the kids to their counselors. When they got home he was yelling at everyone for no evident reason.

"Get a grip!" I snapped when I had finally had enough.

"OH, I forgot that you are perfect! You are the crabby one for yelling at me." He turned all his anger on me.

I didn't like fighting in front of the kids, so I walked away.

"Little miss perfect who never does wrong," Scott yelled after me in his condescending tone.

I just ignored him, got the kids ready for bed, and went to bed myself. He slept on the couch. He would be better in the morning. It could very well be his blood sugars again.

The next morning he left for work without saying goodbye. When he returned in the evening he was still crabby.

We went to our Wednesday evening church service.

A very nice older gentleman approached me after the service: "Ethan was so well-mannered and nice the other day."

"Oh, . . . well, thank you for letting me know!" I replied.

"Scott looked like he was shooting daggers from his eyes into the back of Ethan's head," he then commented.

"Oh, really?!" I replied noncommittaly, playing the stupid card.

"Those kids are really good," the gentleman finished.

"I know. Thank you."

I realized the kids were good. Scott wanted perfection, but that doesn't happen, especially from a seven-year-old boy. I felt that people were noticing Scott's anger more. Some women at church purposely avoided him and made little remarks to me, like, "Oh, is he feeling okay? He seems edgy."

I always had an excuse for Scott's behavior. That was the way he had always been, and I did love him. I just wished he weren't on edge all the time, especially when it came to the kids. Scott had never raised his hands against me, . . . but then, my ex-fiancé hadn't right away, either.

Journal Entry

Why is Scott still mad at me? For sticking up for the kids and myself?

Last week, I took a class on domestic abuse for Stephen Ministry at church. The class brought up for me old memories and feelings but also raised concerns about Scott. Am I really back in an abusive relationship? He seems to be the maddest when he cannot control us. Am I overreacting? Is this normal?

This reminds me of my ex-fiancé, . . . or is everyone's life like this and this is normal? What is normal?

Who do I talk to? My anxiety is building. I feel like I walk on eggshells with a sick feeling in the pit of my stomach all the time. I am constantly in a fight or flight response, waiting for the next thing to drop from the sky. It'll just be a matter of time before anxiety's partner—depression—shows up.

Maybe it's me. I'm not a victim, I bring it upon myself. I have always had someone treating me this way, so it's the way I behave. I piss people off.

If Scott's behavior is normal, though, why are people addressing the issue with me? Should I continue to allow the kids to be scared of Scott? Shouldn't children be somewhat scared of an authoritative parental figure? I don't know what is normal and what isn't.

Self, what do YOU want?

I want Scott to get control of his temper, to not be so stressed out and in turn not to stress out the rest of us. It is hard tiptoeing on pins and needles trying not to set him off.

Where do I go for help, or am I just overreacting? When I bring up his actions it just makes him more irritated. I'm afraid if I seek professional help or help from church it will be like betraying his trust and might ruin my marriage. But if I let it go, it may get ruined anyway. What about the kids?

Scott can be so good, too. He lets me buy what I want— he isn't controlling in that way. Scott controls the checkbook, so he knows what we can afford. He is controlling, though, over how I answer him or talk in a conversation with him.

He is always saying, "Let me finish! You are always interrupting me!"

He stops talking so I think he's done, but I guess there is more to his thoughts. I try to work on it, but I swear I'm not deliberately interrupting.

Scott likes to control what I eat. I will sit on the couch with a bag of chips, and he will stop me and say, "Don't you think you've had enough?" Maybe I am gaining weight.

Scott is always looking for exact wording from the kids too. If it were just me I would find him help professionally. I would take the risk of ruining my marriage. Being that these kids are involved, though, I know that if we got divorced it would be way hard on them, and I couldn't take care of them by myself. Plus if he gets real mad, I wouldn't feel comfortable leaving them with him without me there to redirect his anger at me instead.

If he is open to counseling, it could really help a lot. Change is always scary. So much would change if counseling backfired. That might lead to a divorce. To changes in where I live and in my job and to losing his family members I love, especially Megan.

But there would be no more yelling, no more pins and needles. I'm scared. I'll just stick my head in the sand.

CHAPTER 16

The Blowup

November 15, 2013

A few days later, and I wasn't scared anymore. Maybe God was giving me an answer. I had just sent my last daycare family out the door for the evening. Scott hadn't been home for even ten minutes when he got after Ethan.

"Have you taken your shower?" Scott asked.

"No, I haven't had time," Ethan replied.

"What have you been doing?" Scott asked firmly.

"Watching TV."

"Well, that's not an excuse, is it?" Scott pressed firmly.

"Yeah it is—it's a good excuse," Ethan countered, starting to get upset upon realizing he was in trouble.

This opening argument was partly my fault; I hadn't gotten my nag to Ethan to get his shower done in time. *The sick feeling in my stomach started to rise, along with my pulse.*

Scott started in: "Don't you mouth off to me. There's no reason for you to have not gotten your shower in."

"I just forgot!" Ethan exclaimed. When Ethan is upset his voice goes up an octave.

"I JUST FORGOT!" Scott imitated loudly. Instead of sticking my head in the sand as I usually did, I stood up for Ethan.

"Ethan is only seven and still needs a lot of reminders to do things," I told Scott.

Scott, of course, redirected his anger toward me, which is what I had intended: "OH, I forgot you are a know it all. Why don't you just take care of it all?"

Later that evening we learned that Kayla had forgotten her homework at school. While I was trying to talk to her she went into her "shut down mode," in which she gets throroughly confused, refuses to listen, and concentrates solely on how stupid she thinks she is and how much trouble she is in.

I was trying to get through to her when Scott stepped in with a less than helpful, "Get your head out of your ass."

Obviously we weren't going to reach her that way.

"I'm just stupid!" Kayla cried in anger. "It's not my fault! Stop yelling at me about something I didn't do!"

Scott hated it when the kids talked back!

Scott went over to Kayla quickly. I followed behind, scared of the look in his eye. He started to raise his arm and spin Kayla around to reach her behind.

I was right behind and I grabbed his wrist. "Calm down, Scott. Yelling at them isn't going to help."

He spun around with my hand still on his wrist. "Let go," he scolded from between clenched teeth. I did.

He had that look that my ex-fiancé used to get. The same wild, fiery look associated with being one step away from loss of control.

Scott swore at me a few times, and I sent him outside to start the grill. I sent Kayla to her room to calm down and to get her away from Scott.

As I made dinner Scott kept taking jabs at me: "Maybe you should just do all the parenting, being you're perfect. I'll just shut up and go outside like you want because you always get what you want."

I just ignored him. When I went upstairs to get Kayla for dinner, Scott started in on Ethan downstairs. I went back downstairs and tried to calmly say, "Why don't you take the night off and watch TV upstairs."

Scott threw the spatula that was in his hand at the table. It bounced off the table across the room and onto the floor like a superball. Thankfully, Scott went upstairs.

The rest of the night was peaceful. Erica left for her church group meeting and practically begged me to go with her.

"You're getting yelled at for no reason," Erica pointed out.

"I have to stay to keep the peace," I replied.

Journal Entry

The kids shouldn't be exposed to this. I'm thankful that I have been through this before because I know that I need to stand up for these kids.

Granted, I lose my patience with them. I'm no saint. But I have tried other tactics to approach difficulties, to avoid yelling all the time. Therefore, I have to tell someone. Tonight was scary. It tells me we are getting closer . . . Maybe he will become physical.

Passing of Time

Summer of 2014

Pete passed away from his diabetes. He was only in his fifties. Abigail was devastated. In turn she slipped down into a depression. According to people who know her, it sounded as though she was drinking a lot.

When I told the kids about Pete's passing they seemed to be okay. No one had really talked about Pete. Even Ethan appeared to have no remorse over Pete's death, even though they had gone fishing together a lot. How could they have lived with him for almost a year and not miss him even a little? Abigail moved back to Osceola to be close to her family members.

June 18, 2014

A lot of time had passed since my last journal entry. I hadn't been keeping up on recording my thoughts. I closed my daycare in February 2014 and went to work at a daycare center from March until May, hating every moment of it. I didn't want to reopen my daycare because sharing their space and me was really hard on the kids. There was jealousy and friction between my kids and the daycare kids. It was just easier to shut down the business.

On a recent visit back to Osceola I discussed with Megan our current situation.

"The kids are a handful. They have been through a lot of lies and deceit, trauma, and who knows what else? I feel isolated in Omaha. I wish we could move back here and get help from family members."

"I can't imagine," Megan agreed. "Have you talked to Scott about moving back?"

"Yes. Every time I bring it up he's always worried about how much money he is not going to be making here in Iowa."

"I can see that Scott doesn't handle being told what to do."

"I need to find a different way to talk to him. It must be my tone or the words I use. I need to find a way to make him feel included and not bossed around."

I enjoyed confiding in Megan. She seemed to know Scott well, being that she had been in the family for so long. Plus she was a good friend who listened and lent advice.

I was enjoying my summer off with the kids. In the fall I would be a substitute paraprofessional for the school. The girls were doing great! Erica had shown a lot of maturity that summer. I felt that she and I were starting to develop a relationship. She seemed to trust me more and more and was opening up.

Kayla, though forgetful and disorganized, was showing improvement also. She is a tough cookie.

Kayla liked to reassure me, "I'm not afraid of Scott at all. He knows better than to mess with me!"

Kayla and I had gotten along quite well from the beginning. She called me Mom regularly and was willing to give me hugs and let me know what was happening with her.

Ethan was seeing a psychologist who prescribed anxiety medication. Though he had moments of rage when he was completely out of control of his body, I continued to hold my ground and ignore his bad behavior. I tried hard not to argue back with him.

Ethan wanted to be the one in control, and when he clearly wasn't in that position, he was by default, and in reality, out of control. At eight years old his behavior disturbed me greatly. Sometimes I thought he was acting like he is two- or three-year-old.

Ethan is a really good artist. He had drawn vivid pictures of spiritual warfare, explaining to me that there is a war between God and the devil and claiming that he himself is one of the devil's angels.

"This is the earth. Here are God's angels and here are the devil's angels," he continued as he explained his picture. "There is good and bad. The bad will be cast here, into fire." Ethan pointed to a pit. Maybe they were talking about this in Bible school . . .

"Ethan, I believe you are an angel of God," I told him. "You have the power to decide which side you are on."

A few days later Ethan became so enraged that he picked up a chair from the kitchen table and held it above his head. A different time when he was very angry, he went out to the garage, brought in an axe, and swung it around. Sometimes Ethan scared me even though he was only eight. Maybe he believed he was bad so was playing the part. We would keep seeking help, talking about which voice to listen to, and praying.

CHAPTER 18

Beginning of the End

July 22, 2014

"When you are gone or not looking, Scott hits me," Ethan confided in me one warm summer day.

"What do you mean, hits you?" I asked, seeking clarification.

"I mean he slaps me in the back of the head, or on my chest," Ethan continued. "He did it on our trip to South Dakota, too, and he kicked me when we were alone in the camper."

"WHAT?! Why didn't you tell me sooner, Ethan?"

"I thought you knew," Ethan replied.

I wasn't sure what to say. "I'm sorry that is happening. I will talk to Scott about it."

"No, don't—that's okay," Ethan replied quickly before running off.

Journal Entry

I thought things had gotten better between Ethan and Scott. Scott would just quietly growl at Ethan and not scream at him, at least not in front of me. It appeared that Scott was controlling himself better and that Ethan was listening. Now to find out that Scott has been slapping and kicking Ethan when I'm not around. I'm devastated. I feel at fault because I should have known better. I shouldn't have subjected the kids to this. But where does my allegiance lie? With the man I have been with longer or the children who came later? I already know that answer. The kids have been through enough and don't need this hell added to their lives.

I decided to talk to the counselors to find answers on how to address this issue with Scott without upsetting him too much. I needed to learn how to communicate effectively to him. Maybe I should get my own counselor.

"Scott is getting out of control," I confided to the girls' counselor. "How do I talk to Scott about not pushing Ethan around without Scott blowing up?"

"What do you mean 'pushing Ethan around'?" she probed.

"Well, Scott can be controlling and wants Ethan to act a certain way. When Scott gets too frustrated with Ethan, I guess he hits him," I replied.

"You guess he hits him?" she repeated back to me.

"Yes, I don't see it, as Scott does it when I'm not around. Every time I mention to Scott that he needs to be in better control of his body, he gets upset and it causes a fight. I need to know how to address this to him so I don't upset him," I explained. "Other people have come to me also, concerned about Scott's behavior."

"Oh? Like who?"

"My family, the kids' family, and some church members."

"Well, sounds to me that you don't need to adjust how you communicate to him. Sounds like he has to change the way he behaves."

I nodded in agreement. If only it were that simple.

"You do know that I am a mandatory reporter, right?" she asked.

My heart sank. The sick feeling in the pit of my stomach rose, and the room seemed to spin a little. What had I done?! I wasn't thinking!

"Oh, no! You don't have to report this, do you?" I asked in a panic. *I knew that this would really set Scott off.*

"Yes, I'm afraid I do. I have to make a statement to DHS. It doesn't mean that they will do anything, but it has to be documented," she replied.

"OH, what am I going to do?" I pleaded with tears in my eyes.

"I think you two need to go to counseling yourselves. I have an associate who would be more than willing to work with you. He does parenting and marriage counseling."

"I don't know how I'm going to address counseling with Scott," I replied.

"If you don't tell Scott about the DHS report and counseling, the court will think you're enabling him. They could take the kids away."

That was my worst fear! They couldn't go back into foster care. I had to do this, I could do this. I would do this.

I thanked her for her time and left the office more upset than when I had come in. I was scared to take the first step but knew it needed to be done. I had ignored and hoped for this to go away for too long. *God, help me—I need you so much; please help me! Don't leave me.*

Journal Entry: July 23, 2014

I feel awful. I betrayed Scott. I realize that change has to start somewhere, sometime, and now is the time. I'm scared and have no idea how I'm going to address this mess to Scott. He is going to be so mad.

I know I can't keep pretending this situation will get better. I have to protect my kids. I'm scared of losing my kids, scared of change, of wondering how I'm going to afford housing if I'm on my own. I still love Scott, but I'm not sure I'm IN love with him. I want him to be happy. I care for him. But I need to protect my kids.

I'm terrified of what God says. Marriage is supposed to be forever, so what if divorce seals my fate and God decides I'm not worthy . . . ? That's stupid. He has a plan. Trust and follow Him. I am fearfully and wonderfully made. God loves me.

Scott needs help controlling his temper, figuring out how to show other emotions, and expressing them. Not using anger as a substitute for everything else he feels. Scott wants to be in constant control of everything in life. Ethan and Scott both want control.

Ethan says to Scott and me a lot, "I am going to prove you wrong." He says that even when I praise him and thank him for listening.

Ethan also tells me that "no consequence you try is going to help me. I am never going to listen." However, Ethan still does listen to me. When Scott and Ethan fight, which is every day, it's a constant bickering, invariably followed by a yelling match. Each trying to control the other.

My other fear by myself is that I won't be able to handle Ethan. Scott has shown disrespect to Ethan and me. Ethan won't respect me, being that Scott never has. Or maybe it will be different. I need to find a mentor for Ethan. Ultimately, I hope that Scott will agree to counseling and learn new skills so we can continue as a family. I also hope that through counseling I will learn a few things about myself and how to "grow a pair" for myself and the kids. I need to have a stronger backbone.

CHAPTER 19

My Anchor

July 26, 2014

We went on a little trip and visited my best friend, Darlene. We brought our camper out there and parked it in their driveway. We had a great time visiting, eating, and laughing. They had a small gathering at their house and invited all of Darlene's family. I miss my friend terribly. It is hard being six hours apart.

We have been friends since high school. We have a friendship that you can pick up right where you left off, even though we are six hours apart and don't speak more often than once a month.

Darlene runs little entrepreneurial ventures on the side. Among her many talents are drawing and tattooing. I had her do a small tattoo on the inside of my left wrist. The kids watched as I received my tattoo. They thought it was neat how the needles pierced my skin over and over again. It took only a couple of minutes and it was over. They busily chatted about how they each wanted one too!

"Not until you are eighteen. You want to make sure it's something you can live with for the rest of your life. You don't want to rush any tattoo."

I explained to the kids why I had chosen this symbol: "It's the symbol I see at the altar at church. I find myself fascinated by it. I stare at its design while I pray and feel it helps me have a connection to God. Now that it's on my wrist, it will help me keep focused on God at all times."

I hoped the kids would understand how much thought I had put into this gesture and that there was a meaning behind my tattoo. I had looked up the symbol on the internet earlier. It is a Labarum, also known as a Chi-Rho. *Chi* and *Rho* are the first two letters in the word "Christ" in the Greek language. When put together they represent Jesus.

I had Darlene put it on the inside of my wrist so that I could simply turn my wrist to the side and see the symbol. It would be my anchor, my refuge when I was going through a difficult time. I was excited about my new symbol that would be a part of me forever.

CHAPTER 20

Counseling

August 4, 2014

When we got back from our trip, I knew I had to convince Scott to join counseling with me to work on different parenting techniques. I used the help of a friend at church, John Enner. Scott couldn't get upset with me if the message was coming from someone else.

I explained to John briefly what had been happening, and he agreed to help.

"Scott, sometimes it's helpful to get a little guidance on raising children," John said as we all stood outside the sanctuary at church. "Raising kids is one of the hardest things you'll do, and a little help goes a long way. I know the perfect counselor the two of you could go see."

Scott held John in high respect. John is a strong Christian and one of the first parishioners we met when we joined our church a few years back. "Okay," Scott agreed. "It's worth a shot."

August 18, 2014

We had our first counselor appointment as a couple. Our counselor addressed different issues to do with Ethan.

"Try to have Ethan feel important," the counselor directed. "Don't argue back with him. Give him his consequence and then be done. Don't say anything more."

Scott agreed to this approach and even reflected, "That's a good theory."

"Ethan is young and can't remember all of the rules you have," I felt brave enough to say to Scott in the counselor's presence.

"I'll start looking away more at the dinner table."

This was a great start! It would be hard for him to change, but Scott sounded willing at this time.

I hoped that in the future Scott would keep the same attitude. I knew that by evening the discussion would no longer be fresh in his mind, though. So when I tried to gently remind him I would no doubt get yelled at and told how I think I'm perfect. I may, I conceded, need to find a new way to talk to Scott. Obviously my tone needed to change.

Journal Entry

This week I have been extremely tired. I think I'm becoming depressed. I knew that it was only a matter of time before anxiety's partner in crime would show up. I will pull out of it, though, as I always do. I sure don't need medication to help me. A glass of wine just helps me go to sleep, so I don't need anyone thinking I'm a drunk.

I haven't been sleeping well. Lots of weird dreams about the end of the world and spiders with human heads, big mouths, and nasty teeth . . . and about my living with a different family, a different man, and I'm happy. I question the "message" of the last dream because I'm not sure what it's about.

Maybe I want out of my marriage. I feel that I have to keep trying and shouldn't, as a believer, even consider divorce. What if Scott does change for the better? Will I fall in love with him again? Was I ever in love with him in the first place?

Over our visit I confided in Darlene what was going on.

"I was surprised that you married him at all," she admitted. "I kind of wondered if you were marrying him out of pity."

Maybe Scott and I had totally rushed and hadn't known each other that well. Now here we are—strangers in the same bed.

August 21, 2014

We had another counseling appointment, at which I felt safe enough to put everything on the table. Scott now knew about CPS (Child Protective Services), who it was who had said things about him, and the concerns they had expressed. He didn't seem angry at all as these revelations were expressed. I was impressed at how well he handled it.

That evening, however, Ethan carried the milk carton the wrong way. "Damn it. How many times do I have to tell you to use two hands on the milk?" Scott screamed.

He stopped short immediately. Scott didn't say anything more about it and just went about dinner. He was calm the rest of the evening!

I was happy he wasn't depressed and was being nice to everyone. However, I felt so guilty.

Journal Entry

Today we filled out paperwork about our past for the counselor. Now I feel as though Pandora's Box about has been opened. I thought of things I had buried and didn't want to relive. I turned in the paperwork early to get it out of my mind. I am now filled with anxiety about things that have happened. With all of this, coupled with my depression, I am a hot mess.

I'm irritable, tired, sad, and feeling haunted. Memories invade my thoughts, feelings, and dreams. I wish I could close the box, get past my thoughts. I would love to have a glass of wine and a cigarette now just so I could drown them out. Like I used to.

Old Habits Die Hard

August 22, 2014

I went to the neighbors' for Friday night fun in the driveway. The kids rode bikes in the street, as they did every Friday, and I socialized with the adults. I had a few extra drinks that evening to help drown my thoughts. Scott took the kids inside, and I was alone with neighbors and girlfriends. *I hoped the kids were okay alone with him.*

I bummed a cigarette from someone. I hadn't smoked in a few years. Mostly because Scott had wanted me to quit so badly when we first got together. He had given me an ultimatum: "It's either the cigarettes or me. I can't stand you smelling that way."

I sure didn't want him or the kids finding out what I was doing. The kids would be disappointed in me, and Scott would be furious! The smoke burning my throat felt so good. As I exhaled I got a sense of peace and calm. I was enjoying myself, . . . so I had another drink. Being drunk gave me happier thoughts. Sober, my thoughts tended to have fun with me.

August 23, 2014

I remembered that alcohol is not my friend. Oh, the headache! The kids and I went to an amusement park with the Enner family. I took some Tylenol, drank several cups of coffee, and downed water to rid myself of my self-induced headache before we went. The Enners are God-centered and so brought me back out of darkness throughout the day. Just being around them brought me joy. Hopefully I could stay in the light afterward. I was still irritable but not as dark as I had been the day before.

However, when we got home from the amusement park it was obvious that it was Scott's turn to be dark. Once again I was feeling guilty for having put him there. He opened up that evening.

"I'm having racing thoughts I can't control," Scott stated as we sat on opposite ends of the couch. The kids were in bed after their busy day, so it was a good time to talk.

"I'm having thoughts of you cheating on me." He looked at me accusingly, as though I were doing just that, waiting for me to answer.

"That's not true!" I exclaimed, completely taken aback.

"I know it's not," he admitted, "but I can't help but think that way, being you keep turning me down in bed."

I knew it hurt him that I wanted nothing to do with sex. And, yes, it did have to do with him. It's hard to be intimate with someone who is crabby and grabs body parts when he wants something. Or talks dirty. It makes my skin crawl.

"I'm sorry. I just don't feel like it," I replied evasively. I didn't want to give him the real answer.

He got up and left the room.

When I had given him the real answer in the past it had just upset him. As though he were angry with me or maybe with himself. Down on himself, as though he felt unattractive. I had asked him to tell me he loved me, give me a kiss, or even just touch or rub my arm. Instead I would get butt-slapping, boob-grabbing "I want to take advantage of you." This tells me what an undeserving piece of meat I've always been. *I'm messed up. Everyone is broken, so suck it up, move on, and let God. Why is that so hard?*

August 25, 2014

It had been a few days, and my extended family members had gone off on a tangent again about my marriage. "You deserve better, Heather. You need to open your eyes."

Now another friend wanted to talk in the afternoon. I knew she was going to give me a piece of her mind, too. I just didn't want to hear it.

"Heather, I'm concerned about you and the kids. You all seem so unhappy. Let me know if there is anything I can do." I just smiled, nodded, and said "Thank you."

Journal Entry

Maybe I should move on, but I care about Scott and don't want to hurt him. I am already hurting him and the kids with my crabby self. I feel helpless. I'm getting blue again and feeling sorry for myself. Stop it. Take control. Be the bitch. Act happy—you can do it.

"Self, are you happier when Scott isn't around? What triggers your irritation?"

I reply to myself with answers: "Kids arguing, I'm not getting enough space. Disrespect. I'm selfish. Maybe I need to show more respect so I can earn more respect."

I feel the kids are treating me and each other more disrespectfully. I'm more disrespectful to others than I used to be. I don't feel like putting up with as much crap as I used to. Is that being disrespectful to others, or maybe I'm having more respect for myself . . .

August 28, 2014

After the kids went to bed, Scott and I had a serious heart-to-heart as we sat on the living room couch. I told him about all the demons haunting me. "I have discovered that I used to feel safe with you, but I no longer do. My trust is gone." I mustered enough courage to get it out.

"I understand that. I have hurt you. I want you to do what will make you happy, Heather," Scott replied.

I have no idea what that is. I have always been more concerned for everyone else and what they need or how they will feel. I know that he loves me and will do anything to make me happy. So if I don't feel the same way, the least I can do is make him happy by being with him. I'm so selfish for not loving him back the same way. I can't hurt him; he already hurts.

"No matter what happens, I will financially support my family and give you whatever you need, even if we are not together. You deserve to be happy and do what is best for you," Scott acknowledged. "Of course I want you to be with me and that would make me happy, but do what's best for you, not for me or the kids."

I can't do that! I always put everyone else first. It's not in me to think about myself. I want to do what's best for the kids. He is being so nice! I want Scott to be happy. He is so anxious and depressed. I hurt him. I'm so selfish.

There were a few minutes of silence as we sat on the couch. "Do you know what you want to do?" Scott asked.

I don't know! I need time to see if things will work, to gain trust back. Try not to think of myself and think more of his needs. Stop being selfish. I have to be strong. No more feeling sad about this. It's hard on the kids. Don't let them see you are sad. Stop. Now. Scott is sad and anxious enough. You can only control yourself. If you're the strong role model, they will follow. I feel so fake.

"No, I don't know," was all that I could squeak out to Scott for an answer.

"I'm going to leave a card on the table in the morning," Scott said. "I want you to text me in the morning one of three words: 'relevant,' 'irrelevant,' or 'wait.' I want to know if the card is too late for me or if it's okay to say what I want to say. Text 'wait' if you need more time."

"Okay," I replied. I thought I understood his request. We slept in separate rooms again.

CHAPTER 22

Reforming

August 29, 2014

Scott left for work early in the morning and left his note with a card on the table. It stated that he was going to change and stop trying to create a perfect family. He listed off good traits about everyone in the family.

There was no apology. This was a start for him, acknowledging that we deserved better and pledging that he was going to try. I texted him "relevant" because I was giving him the chance to redeem and to see whether we could still patch things up.

I asked Erica what she thought of the card. Her body language was a cringe. She finally did say, "I like it, but I don't think he will change."

That evening Scott asked me, "Who is the card relevant to?"

I was so confused.

"It's relevant to all of us working on this together," I explained.

He seemed disappointed. I believe Scott thought this letter would make things better more quickly. Was it supposed to? Or was I just being a bitch and holding a grudge?

Journal Entry

I agree with Erica and believe Scott may not change, either, but I am not willing to give up yet. How selfish am I to expect him to change, when I can't love him if he doesn't? Yet he loves me despite all my imperfections and is willing to sacrifice everything for me. So I will stay with him to make him happy. That is my sacrifice.

Journal Entry: September 23, 2014

A month later and we are seeing our counselor every two weeks. We are also still receiving mentoring from our church friends, the Enners. I'm listening to CDs on forgiveness and on how to help Scott step up to manhood. The CDs talk about choosing maturity for myself, speaking the truth in love, praising Scott when he steps up, believing that Scott can be godly, and pursuing godliness within myself.

I'm having problems with speaking truth. Scott doesn't receive it well. Scott thinks I'm treating him like a child.

Sometimes I am guilty of that because he is acting like one. I don't want the confrontation, so I stick my head in the sand.

I'm also having problems believing in him. I feel that he isn't going to change. I feel that he doesn't want to change and is only going to counseling to pacify me. He doesn't see the long-term benefits. Scott wants things to be better now.

I need to ask for forgiveness in order to give forgiveness. Healing doesn't come before you choose to forgive. It comes afterward. You can heal only after you let go of the anger and give forgiveness.

I had my usual internal conversation with myself:

"I'm sorry for letting bad things happen to you. I'm sorry for being passive and for not letting myself get close to God. I will stop putting me down," I apologized to myself.

"I forgive myself," I responded back.

I feel a little better. As I continue to work on my forgiveness of myself, I believe I may be close to forgiving Scott. I see him trying and am starting to see changes in him. I am so excited.

Journal Entry: September 25, 2014

A few days later I'm sitting at the table on the deck in the warm afternoon fall sunshine. The kids went to the park to play, and Scott is still at work. I enjoy my quick quiet times. I can hear the wind rattling through the fall leaves as I read my Bible and try to hold the pages open as they keep trying to blow upward with the wind.

I absentmindedly read John 15:7–8: "If you remain in me and my words remain in you, ask whatever you wish, and it will be done for you. This is to my Father's glory, that you bear much fruit, showing yourselves to be my disciples."

I flashed in my imagination to having a baby after sharing with everyone that this was impossible, all the while knowing that nothing is impossible with God and that performing the "impossible" allows Him to showcase His glory. I immediately reverted to feeling selfish and retracted the suggestion: "NO, GOD! That is not what I want! A baby?!" Tears ran down my cheeks. Wanting a baby has truly not been on my mind.

The sun came out from behind the clouds and warmed my skin. The breeze blew gently through the fall leaves as they rattled a tune. I could feel Him. I apologized to God and asked for forgiveness for my temper tantrum.

This is the second time it has pressed on my heart heavily that I am going to have a baby. The first was at the counselor's while Scott was talking, I don't remember what about. The internal dilemma I was having with myself had to do with sleeping arrangements! WEIRD! It was a quick image of a baby, somehow in conjunction with the month of March. I then was worried about where to put the baby. I'm not sure whose voice it is, God's or the enemy's.

CHAPTER 23

Answers and Small Worlds

October 1, 2014

I started my new job at Pine Schools, a coed alternative school. I worked with very troubled teenagers and often wondered if that would have been the way Kayla turned out had she not come into our care. I say Kayla because she has more spunk than Erica does.

I started working with an eighteen-year-old young man. He had some anger issues, but we had a connection. He came to me and talked to me about his problems. He reminded me a lot of Ethan—just an older version of him. The young man had trust issues, could not take no for an answer, and had a felt need to be in control. I asked the lead teacher at the end of the day, "What is the young man's diagnosis?"

She replied, "He has reactive attachment disorder."

October 7, 2014

I visited with Ethan's psychiatrist, Dr. Michael, for medication. We had tried all sorts of medication with Ethan. I felt as though Ethan could just be his guinea pig.

Ethan was able at this appointment to express the turmoil in his head. When he was having a temper tantrum in his room he was actually hitting his head on the floor and wall and stabbing pencils into his skin. He hated everyone, including himself. When he was told no it sent him into a tailspin. Dr. Michael understood Ethan's felt need to be in control.

"Ethan wants to discipline himself when he is acting up, so he hits himself, giving him back the control," he explained.

I had Ethan go to the waiting room to wait for me and proceeded to ask Dr. Michael, "Could Ethan have reactive attachment disorder?"

Dr. Michael looked at me in disbelief and asked, "Do you think you are a terrible mother?"

I looked at him, puzzled. "Do you look at your notes often? Ethan is adopted."

I then proceeded to explain to him AGAIN that Ethan had been with us for only a few years, along with Ethan's background.

Dr. Michael exclaimed, "Yes, that's exactly what he has! I kept ruling out reactive attachment disorder and not considering it a possibility because I could see you are a good mother."

I felt honored by the compliment but extremely frustrated that we had been spinning in circles for so long because the psychiatrist couldn't remember that Ethan was adopted. The struggles with mental health care inadequacies in the system are real. Dr. Michael then proceeded with his ideas for new medication. A new rollercoaster for poor Ethan.

October 8, 2014

Our marriage counselor touched on the difference between trust and forgiveness: "Just because you forgive someone doesn't mean you need to trust them."

That was enlightening. I felt as though he was directing that statement to me. Sometimes it seemed as though he was specifically trying to tell me something.

October 9, 2014

In the morning Ethan drew me a picture of an event that had been in his mind. It included a rising sun with the devil's eye and blood.

"The devil goes inside me. There are a lot of troubles in the world," Ethan explained. "There is a constant war. The Holy Spirit comes and sends all the demons to hell."

Ethan has amazing insight into the spiritual world. We needed to discuss with him further about which voices to listen to. Scott believed that Ethan's expressed insights were God showing us our window of opportunity to reach him. I believed he was right.

God, continue to bless us and show us your will as we continue on this new spiritual journey. I hope to someday show this journaling to individuals I love so they can join us on this quest of life and find eternal life with you. Amen.

October 14, 2014

Over the weekend the kids stayed with Kyle and Megan while Scott and I spent eighteen hours away at a hotel and went to a murder mystery dinner. The kids enjoyed staying with Kyle and Megan so they could hang out with Ryker and Kelly.

It sounded as though they had a great time with Ryker and Kelly, getting into all kinds of mischief. Ryker and Ethan played video games, while Kelly, Erica, and Kayla painted nails and did each other's hair.

When we went to pick up the kids, we were in the backyard visiting with Kyle and Megan and all the kids.

As we stood there visiting our kids, they yelled out "SAVANNAH!" and took off running up the hill. There stood Collin's black Labrador on the top of the hill. Just walking around the truck was Collin.

We all started up the hill toward Collin and Savannah. As we talked to Collin, he asked the kids, "How did you know this was Savannah? She looks like any black lab, and you wouldn't have known that I moved here."

"Oh, we always recognize Savannah!" they exclaimed. Collin had just bought a house, ironically only a few houses from Kyle and Megan. What a small world!

We headed for home shortly afterward. Soon anxiety, crabbiness, meltdowns, and mouthing back resumed. This was why we didn't often get away. Change was hard on the kids. I got that, but I had a life, too.

Journal Entry

I feel that I am the one who has to pick up everyone's pieces. So and so is having a hard time. They are sad, have anxiety, or feel inadequate or angry about something, so they all bring it to me. Show it to me. Expect me to handle it. Even with God's help I'm having a hard time.

When do I get my meltdown? My angry moment? My sad? When I do lose my cool no one helps me pick up the pieces. They mirror my feelings instead. What the hell? I'm not supposed to mirror yours but pick up the pieces and make it better? What about my pieces? In addition, I take on your burdens plus my own. No one takes on my burdens. The world is on my shoulders, and I have no human to help lighten my load.

I have God, though. Please, God, take my load off my shoulders. Give me strength to take on all the family's burdens. Help me not to have a meltdown. Give me wisdom to not act like a fool when the rest of my family is doing just that. Help me show you to them so they can rely more on you and not me.

CHAPTER 24

The Art of Fake Smiling

October 15, 2014

Abigail informed us that Stacy was back in the Osceola area. She was trying to clean up her act, so she had moved back to the area for family support. Trying to juggle schedules around the kids' biological mom was going to be tricky.

I was happy that Stacy was back in her family's life. Stacy needed them, and they needed her. However, it would make it really hard on us having to tiptoe around Osceola. We probably wouldn't be back there as often. I couldn't be selfish, though. I was happy she was getting better, and I prayed that she might find you, Lord.

October 18, 2014

We had a birthday party for Kayla at a local restaurant in Osceola. The kids' biological family made it: Abigail, the aunts, and Kenneth, Marie, and Collin. I was a little nervous about getting together with the kids' family, as I didn't want any unexpected or unwelcome visitors showing up. I was putting my trust in Abigail.

We put on our fake smiles and made it through. Of course, there were pictures galore with Marie! The kids always got their pictures taken with her and the family. Theirs was the first stable home they had experienced.

I was anxious the whole time, wondering if Scott was going to hold it together. Meals were always hard with him and Ethan. Scott had been very edgy during the week since our weekend outing together. I was wondering if he was questioning our adoption. He kept implying how nice it had been with just the two of us.

Journal Entry: October 27, 2014

This weekend was rough, with overtired girls from long nights of sleepovers and a confirmation retreat. I am depressed and not wanting to be a mom again. It gets so bad that I don't even want to get close to my Bible or a journal when I get depressed. I need to get over myself, open them up, and get close to you, Lord. To remember that all feelings, thoughts, and situations are temporary. Everything is temporary. Life in this world is temporary.

I'm happy to be resting back in His shadow tonight. I am so thankful and astonished at how much God has transformed

Scott and in such a short time. He is calm and respectful to the kids, and we all seem to be getting along. Except that Ethan still has upsets. I really pray that we continue to grow together in our faith and become stronger as a married couple. We are proof of wonderful things God can do.

Keep helping me, Lord, to show Ethan yourself and to do your will, not mine. Help me to help Ethan feel you and grow closer to you, God. Please don't let me and my selfish ways get into your way. Show me creative ways to help Ethan cope with life, loose the grip of the enemy, and grow closer to you.

Journal Entry: November 5, 2014

I became too boastful. I became greedy, wanting to see more from God. The last couple of days I felt as though God had left me, when truly He never did. He was showing me that what He is giving me now is enough. To be patient. I'm starting to see by faith, and therefore walk by faith and be thankful that God is enough and is giving enough.

Poor Ethan is having a terrible time. I must walk by faith that God will provide for him. Don't let me be in the way of your will, Lord. I only want to protect the kids and provide. However, isn't that your job? Don't let me be in the way.

Try to be an assertive Christian. Speak the truth, but in love and get rid of stinking thinking!

I asked myself, "Do you spend more time and effort providing, handing out, and following through on consequences?

Or do you have more time set up for providing God's love, support, and encouragement? Do the children spend more time dealing with punishment or experiencing God's love?"

I don't like the answers I have for those questions.

November 29, 2014

We decided not to go to Thanksgiving with the kids' family due to Stacy's being in the area. We heard that the kids' aunt wasn't going to the gathering either and safely assumed that Stacy would be there.

My neighbor friend called me: "Hi, Heather."

"Hey, how's it going?"

"Well . . . I'm actually calling in regards to an incident our neighbor from across the street saw the other evening."

"OH?!" I asked, caught off guard. I wondered what gossip she had for me!

"Yeah, this neighbor confided in me about the incident because he knew we were friends." My heart sank, realizing, *This incident involves me. It can't be good.*

"Is now a good time for us to come over to visit?" she asked. "I mean, is Scott gone?"

"Yes, he's at work," I was able to squeak out.

Once she knew that Scott was at work, my friend and the neighbor from across the street both came over to my house.

"I saw Scott and Ethan out delivering Christmas wreaths together," the neighbor from across the street explained uncomfortably.

"Ethan did something wrong—I'm not sure what. I think it had to do with dropping a wreath. I saw Scott spank him, but not a regular spank." He paused.

"What do you mean?"

"Scott used excessive force. His arm circled around. Like he was winding up swinging a bat. It wasn't just a swat on the butt. It wasn't just once, either. It was like five times. I found it very disturbing. I have seen the way he talks to the kids, too. It's not healthy."

It was the same song and dance I had heard from others. Scott was good at hiding things from me and manipulating me to think things were changing. He kept saying that he hadn't been hitting Ethan, but the kids had been reporting otherwise. I didn't know who to believe. Maybe that was why Ethan had been acting up. Secretly Scott had been hitting Ethan again behind my back? Scott appeared to have changed, but was he just doing that to impress me?

I wanted to throw up.

"I don't know what to do," I responded. "We are in counseling."

"Heather, we are worried about you. We feel that you and the kids are not safe," my friend concluded.

CHAPTER 25

Terrified

November 30, 2014

I went to an abuse shelter. Being that there had been no substantiated case of Scott's abusing Ethan or me, they could not house us. They gave me a plan instead.

"This is what you need to do," the intake coordinator explained. "Pack a bag with extra clothes and whatever else you may need. Start taking money out of your bank accounts. If you do this a little at a time it won't be as noticeable. Keep this all stashed away at a safe person's house. Get it out of your house. Don't keep it in a car, either. You want to do this in case you need to flee quickly. Do you think he will get physical?"

"NO, I don't think so," I replied nervously. I really didn't think Scott would hit me, but I guessed it could happen.

"Does he have any weapons in the house?" she asked.

"No," was my first response, . . . but then I remembered. "Yes! Scott has a couple shot guns."

"Okay. Take those out of the house as well and keep them in a safe place. You don't want him getting access to weapons just in case," the intake coordinator replied. "Good luck."

I went home and packed a bag. In it I put my own clothes, along with an outfit from each child's room. I went to the bank and withdrew cash. Enough to get by for now. I brought it over to my neighbor friend's house. I also went back and found all the guns I could think of and brought them to the neighbor across the street. I found only two guns. I thought that was all.

I didn't know what was going to happen. I didn't have a plan for what to do next. I was terrified. Terrified of change, terrified of him, terrified of the next day and of the days to follow. Breathe. Just Breathe. One minute at a time. Breathe.

December 13, 2014

I was so upset with how things were going. A dark voice inside me was on a rampage as I cleaned the house, frantically trying to cope with my thoughts.

"It's getting closer to Christmas, and everything is a bunch of crap. The more you show love to your family, the more you make yourself vulnerable. More opportunity for them to shit on you. All your life you have shown love, empathy, and compassion for others. For what? To be shit on. Constantly.

Bullied from childhood to adolescence. Nicknamed in high school 'Butter Face.' 'Everything looks good on you but your face, Butter Face.'

I cleaned the toilet harder. Trying to scrub away the pain.

"In college you tried to fit in and be loved," the voice continued. *"Ruined, abused again by your ex fiancé, your 'one true love.' Alcohol. You were so happy drunk all those years, hopping from one bed to another. At least you were numb. Then what? Stupid you. You thought you should move forward and better yourself. You found Scott."*

"I found God," I protested.

"At least you thought you found God," the dark voice continued. *"You were somewhat happy but wanted to be home closer to your family. Idiot. You thought a baby would do that and bring you home. You thought kids would change it all. Maybe it would have, but you're a moron and could not wait. Let's adopt three kids! You're a superhero! What an idiot. The kids don't love you. They only want what they can get without a care about anyone else or how it affects others."*

"The counselors are always saying 'Don't take it personally,'" I tried to reassure myself.

"It's too late! That's all you have ever done!" The dark voice was now yelling. *"Take the weight of the world on your shoulders trying to care for others. Trying to love, do what is good. For what!? To be shit on!"*

I left the bathroom and headed for the living room.

"God is leading you." I heard the small whisper.

"He doesn't exist! Maybe he did die. You are sure not with Him now," the dark voice taunted.

"Maybe I would be better off gone," I thought. *"They all would be better off without me."*

I was absentmindedly dusting. Moving things off shelves but totally focused on my thoughts.

"They don't need you. Scott can handle it. They wouldn't have your negativity around them anymore. You wanting to give up. Just give up. Run away," the dark voice continued.

I can't drown it out. Tears flooded my eyes.

"I may just go home. God will not accept me home after these awful thoughts of Him not existing. I wonder, if I make my suicide an accident if the kids would forgive me, not worry and then forget me. Move on."

My thoughts turned to what the dark voice was telling me. I couldn't see clearly through the tears.

"All I want to do is sleep. Go home. Will You bring me home, Lord? Should I try to come home?"

"NO, STOP!" Again the small whisper.

"It's easier than running away. Then I don't have to worry about money or being found. I'm just gone. Closure for all and then . . . I'm just a memory."

My thoughts morphed into the dark voice.

There is no hope. I can't even cry anymore—just angry, sad, . . . gone. Leave on your own. Accidentally. Or I could go see the mountains . . .

Fall asleep in the garage with the car running. I could leave work early. I should do it after Christmas. I don't want to ruin Christmas for others. Maybe my birthday. I think it would be cool to be born and die on the same date. It would look cool on your tombstone.

My movement slowed, and so did the tears.

I realized it would have to be an accident for life insurance to pay out. I would have to get insurance to pay for my death; then Scott would be set and could move closer to home and get help from his family. Please get the money so Scott and the kids will be okay. Be sure they don't see my journaling, though—don't tell. What are my options?

Hanging is definitely not an accident.

Car accident. I don't want others involved. I can look for a bridge or ramp, be unstrapped, and lean over the seat like I'm picking something up or changing the radio station or texting and oops! Over.

I don't really want to drown. Always been scared of that.

Or fire—don't care to burn, either. Guess I'd rather drown.

What else? Farm equipment. Hard to start running that on my own, though.

Accidental drug overdose? How do you prove that was an accident?

No more tears. It's time to harden your heart. Stick your heart in a metal box.

CHAPTER 26

Depressed

December 24, 2014

I was able to quiet the dark voice. It came and went, though some days were worse than others.

It was Christmas Eve, and I was supposed to sing a solo at church. On the way there, Ethan was upset about presents. He wanted to open his right away. He got so upset about not getting his way that he started kicking Scott's seat while he drove.

Scott got so upset that he was swinging his arms behind him violently, trying to get Ethan to stop. I think Scott was trying to hit Ethan. So Ethan turned it into a game and proceeded to keep kicking Scott's seat harder, while swinging his legs to avoid Scott's arms. All the while we were all yelling at each other to stop and threatening to cancel Christmas. Yay, family!

We got to the service miraculously without a car accident. I sang my solo but sure wasn't feeling the spirit of Christmas. This was not how I had pictured my family. We were so distant from each other. Scott and Ethan were both out of control. I couldn't keep doing this. I was supposed to sing at the midnight service too. I texted the choir director at 10:00 p.m., asking her to fill in for me. I was far too depressed to sing.

January 1, 2015

New Year's 2015: I wanted to have a private gathering with Abigail and the kids so they could have Christmas together. Abigail wanted to know times and dates and was pushing for a specific time. At the last minute I changed it to a few hours later, arranging to meet at her house instead of in public.

During our visit Erica was playing on Abigail's cell phone when Stacy texted multiple times, asking if the kids were still there and demanding pictures and cards. This told me that even though I had given Abigail a few hour window, she had still turned around and told Stacy when we were coming. It was hard on Erica seeing those texts come through. Kayla said that this had happened to her, too. It was hard on them that they couldn't trust Abigail and that she wouldn't allow them to move on.

Abigail had no problem lying to me. I believed she was not putting the kids first. I felt that, given that she was putting Stacy and herself before the kids, it was wise that we stop seeing her for their mental health.

I felt betrayed because Abigail had already been on thin ice for Christmas, and then she had let Stacy know our plans. Yet Abigail claimed that she and Stacy didn't get along. Then she gave Erica her phone, knowing that Stacy would text. This relationship was ending. The kids could make their own choices in the future. I was doing the best I could, trying to give them stability and someone they could depend on. This was in their best interest.

I was spending a few days at a cabin by myself. Scott was at work in Omaha, and I separated the kids and sent them to different family members. One to Kyle and Megan, one to Russell, and one to my parents.

Christmas was awful, and our functionality as a family was grim. Something needed to change. I couldn't think and reflect while everyone was around. Our family members seemed more than happy to each take a kid over Christmas break for a few days. I didn't think anyone was aware or alarmed that something was afoot.

No one knew that I was at a cabin except for Scott. I needed to figure out what we were doing.

I start my internal dialogue with *"Is this a failed adoption? Do we need to send the kids back to Abigail? Is this more than we can handle? Or is this a failed marriage? Am I giving up too quickly?"*

We kept attending counseling, but the situation didn't seem to be getting better. I was so depressed. I just needed to relax and reflect and figure out what we were going to do. Help me, Lord! I spend my days thinking, praying, and binge watching *Criminal Minds*.

January 10, 2015

Back in Omaha, I attended a women's retreat at church. It was a nice overnight getaway on my own, but I couldn't help but find myself secluded and thinking about the kids and whether they were doing okay with Scott. I needed God so badly that I went anyway to get away and clear my head.

I had been pretty dark a month earlier, when I had felt as though I would have been better off dead. I didn't want to go back there. I needed answers, though, on what to do.

We discussed and meditated on 2 Corinthians 4:7–9: "But we have this treasure in jars of clay to show that this all-surpassing power is from God and not from us. We are hard pressed on every side, but not crushed; perplexed, but not in despair; persecuted, but not abandoned; struck down, but not destroyed."

This spoke to me. We have treasures or gifts from God, either as a power or as a personality trait. Even though we are troubled, nothing can take these gifts away.

CHAPTER 27

The End

January 12, 2015

Ethan and Scott were having an argument in the bathroom about the toilet not being flushed and cleaned up. I walked by the bathroom quietly, in time to see Scott's arm swing back and then thrust full forward right into Ethan's chest. I lost it.

I grabbed Ethan and got him out of the bathroom. I took him into his room and closed the door. I looked at Ethan's chest. He had a red mark that looked like a handprint. I gave him a hug as he cried. I laid Ethan in his bed. He calmed down and started looking at books. I left his room and found Scott in the living room.

I screamed at him, "THIS IS ENOUGH. I CAN'T DO THIS ANYMORE!" and stormed away before he could respond. An overwhelming sense of strength came over me as I realized I had to get the kids out of this situation. I went upstairs to the bedroom, shook, and wept. I was positive this incident wasn't the first time since the previous fall, when Ethan and Scott had been delivering wreaths.

I knew that Scott wasn't going to change. I couldn't let this keep happening to the kids—and especially to Ethan. I couldn't live like this any longer. Our situation had to change. It was going to change. My marriage was over.

Scott and I went a few days without speaking to each other. Scott hid in the bedroom or in the basement. The kids and I did our own thing. I finally mustered enough strength to confront him.

"We need to talk," I announced in a monotone.

"Oh yeah, what . . . ?"

"I want a separation," I blurted as fast as I could. "We need a break from each other, and you need a break to figure out what is important to you." My heart was beating so loudly I swore Scott could hear it too.

"Well, I'm not moving out, so I guess you will have to," Scott replied with a stone cold face.

"Fine."

I walked away. I was not backing down, even though I was shaking. For the first time in my life I felt empowered. Strong. Even though I trembled with anxiety, I knew I had to protect my kids.

I started asking around for a place the kids and I could go. The Enner family was the first to offer us a place to stay. I knew I needed that family to keep me strong and close to God.

John asked whether he could talk to Scott first, though. I agreed. Later that day Scott came home. The kids and I were already in the process of packing. Scott stopped me.

"Hey, I got to thinking. It would be better for me to leave. I am only one person, and instead of uprooting the kids and your routine, it would be easier for me to go. I'm going to stay with the Enner family. I asked them if I could stay there."

I knew exactly what had happened. John had talked to him and convinced him of what he should do. Scott must have thought I was stupid.

"Okay, I think that's a great idea. Thank you," I replied. I decided not to call him out on his crap and cause a fight.

The next day the kids went to school, I went to work, and Scott moved out with some of his clothes while we were gone.

January 26, 2015

A week later the kids seemed more relaxed, and, honestly, I was too. Ethan had thrown only had a couple of tantrums, and they were not nearly as long lasting as they had been.

In the meantime Scott claimed that he'd had some epiphany and was going to change. I prayed, for his soul, that this was the truth. I knew God had the power and authority to change Scott. However, I was not waiting around. I was fully aware that it was possible for Scott to change, but I also recognized that a transition would take years. He had always been like this, and I didn't have that many more years with the kids. Scott's behavior was like an addiction that he would have to keep working on day after day.

For the time being, Scott agreed to be supervised by someone when he was with the kids. The Enners, Pastor Danica, and a neighbor had all agreed to help with that.

I have a very soft heart that felt sad for Scott, but I had to be strong. I kept vacillating back and forth between wanting a divorce and worrying that I was prematurely giving up. I couldn't discern what God wanted me to do but do know that God sees divorce as detestable.

I kept sending mixed messages to the kids because I was so wishy-washy about what I should be doing. Should we get divorced or just separate?

Pastor Danica said to me in a private meeting, "In order to move forward with a divorce you will have to harden your heart. The trick is not to let the hardening consume you, though."

She continued, "Now you have to see this process as evil that needs to be stopped."

I needed to be strong. I started my internal conversation back at home where it was quiet. *"The difference in emotions is that when I feel like what I'm doing is right I feel strong, at peace, happy, joyful, and hopeful. Then when I waiver and question what I'm doing, I feel hopeless, in turmoil and pain—the same pain I've been feeling for years."*

"Which feeling would be God?" I asked myself. "The Peace, Hope, Joy," was the obvious answer.

"Then you are doing the right thing. You are getting a divorce for the sake of the kids. You are so strong. You want to hear 'Well-done, faithful servant.' Stop walking on the fence and stay on your side of it. God is in control, and He is taking care of all of us. He will never lead us astray," I assured myself.

CHAPTER 28

Torn and Confused

February 1, 2015

Things had been going well. The kids had been making huge changes and were more relaxed. I was too. The kids and I went with Pastor Danica and her kids to their cabin over the weekend. All of them got along great. We had a great, peaceful time making candles and tea, and the kids went ice-skating on the lake.

I had gone to a lawyer and started the paperwork process. My parents were helping me out greatly. They not only gave me the motivation to go to the lawyer but went along with me. The lawyer was not stunned over reports of Scott's behavior.

"Oh, honey. You are well educated, young, and pretty. You will marry again," he blithely assured me.

HA! WHATEVER!

"Just be sure you choose more wisely," he concluded.

Journal Entry
John Enner had blessed me with a lot of CDs to listen to. Along with the marriage counselor, he was helping Scott and me maneuver through what we were going to do. I took notes as I listened.

Remarriage
Situations in which God allows remarriage:

1. *Matthew 19:8—unrepentant, immoral partner, hardening takes time.*
2. *1 Corinthians 7:8–15—desertion by unbelieving mate.*
3. *2 Corinthians 5:16–17—marital failure prior to salvation; married for wrong reasons.*

February 8, 2015
The kids sat with Scott at church, and there appeared to be no anxiety.

I felt compelled to spend time with him today, or at least have the kids do so. However, I didn't have anyone to supervise, so we went out to eat together. To my surprise, I felt good letting him come over to the house to play games. The kids and Scott played a board game and Nerf guns. They all had a great time and hopefully made some memories.

Scott said as he was leaving, "Thanks for letting me come over. How am I ever going to be able to show you

I have changed or am improving if you don't give me chances?"

I saw where he was coming from, but was it just another manipulative move to get to us? Was I being too secular and listening more to society than to God?

He was being nice now, but until when? Would that cycle repeat in the future? We'd been through this before. "I'm sorry. I'm all better. It won't happen again" takes hold for a few weeks, and then—BOOM!—the bliss is over.

While Scott was there the kids did act a little strangely. More high-strung again and fidgety. After he had gone we all felt calmer, happier, and less anxious. I did care for Scott and wanted the best for him. By the same token, I'm quite sure *we* are not the best for him.

I felt terrible for the girls. They didn't trust men. They had no idea how a man should treat them. Ethan, from his side, had no model for how to treat a woman or his future kids. *I know you are here, God, holding my hand. I wish and pray I could discern your voice over all the other voices.*

Journal Entry

Looking back over my journaling today, I realized again that when I met Scott I was just giving up drinking and my old party life. I had believed that Scott was a reward, only to learn later on that he was in fact another lesson. I believe that if or when we get divorced I will never remarry, unless Scott gets called home. The Bible clearly states that in God's eyes we are forever married.

However, if I had truly understood God's intentions for marriage I would never have married Scott. We had married for the wrong reasons.

Pastor Danica spoke to me about being unequally yoked: "Do not be yoked together with unbelievers. For what do righteousness and wickedness have in common? Or what fellowship can light have with darkness?" (2 Corinthians 6:14).

I was so conflicted. What if I somehow miraculously met my Boaz (referring to the biblical book of Ruth)? Would I remarry? I do realize that divorce is hated by God and that it is not his intention, but I also believe that divorce under given circumstances can be permissible. If I did not remarry, I might stand a chance to enter His kingdom.

I do hope to be able to at least get into heaven. I don't need a special place prepared, Lord. I can be out on the streets of gold. I don't want to be cast into the fiery pits of hell. I guess I'd rather stay married and ruin the kids than go to hell; maybe that is your will . . . ?

February 10, 2015

I was still working at the alternative school and learning daily from the actions of the young man with reactive attachment disorder what to do and not do with Ethan.

In my free time I googled Iowa and tried to figure out where we would be going when we moved back. I wanted a town with a good school, close to my family, but not too close due to the biological family members. I knew that the biological family would inevitably find out that we are back in the area, and I was leery of having them show up at my doorstep.

I was also looking for a centrally located town so that it would be easy to commute to a job in a bigger town, if needed. After a few days of research, I kept falling back on the same town over and over again. I felt comfortable that this was where we needed to go: Leon, Iowa. I believed God was leading me there.

February 14, 2015

Scott had been served his divorce paperwork the day before. At the same time, he had left with the kids and his family for a snowmobiling trip. In our paperwork and by discussion with Pastor Danica, Scott and I had reached an agreement that his family would supervise him whenever he had the kids. This was for my own peace of mind, allowing me to trust that the kids were being taken care of and that he wasn't totally losing his cool.

I wished I had documented more of his outbursts. If only I had called the police when he'd had episodes, all of this history would have been documented and the preventative steps easier to enforce. I had been protecting Scott at the time, thinking I could change him.

Now I had to protect the kids, but in turn I would have to pay the price for not having called the police and gotten his abuse documented.

I trusted that his family would keep him supervised and that there would be no issues. I missed them already, especially Megan. I really hoped he had brought the papers with him and that together they would look them over. I also hoped that he would find the provisions reasonable and just sign the papers so we could all move on.

On Monday I hoped to go to the town of Leon, Iowa, to look at houses. I prayed that his family would talk him into letting us move to Iowa in order to have the support we all needed. I didn't really understand what was special about Leon but felt myself drawn there.

CHAPTER 29

The Drama

February 25, 2015

We saw Scott over the weekend at church. He let it be
known that he might not allow us move to Iowa. He
wanted me to stop the divorce so we could make the
move together as a family. Then, if we wanted, we could
continue the divorce in Iowa.

He said that we could move to different towns but
attend the same church in Iowa. I was livid! That would
have been so weird! *Please help me discern, Lord. Help me
recognize manipulation and deceit, truth and change. How
is Scott going to act when he moves out of the Enner home?*

March 7, 2015

Scott and I talked over the phone. "Why don't you cancel
the divorce and you can move to Iowa tomorrow," he
suggested.

"Whatever! You would turn around and get me for
kidnapping," I pointed out.

"If you wanted to move to Iowa so bad, we could have moved a year ago if you would just have said you were leaving," Scott countered.

What a load of crap! I had tried talking him into moving to Iowa numerous times.

"I was still trying to save the marriage at that time and wouldn't have moved without you. You were always more worried about how much money you were making."

"I don't want you moving because I want to be a dad."

If that were the case, then why in the last month or so when I had made arrangements for him to see the kids had he not attended some of the events he had been invited to? I believe that Scott didn't want us moving to Iowa because he wouldn't have been able to control us there.

"Well, you should have been a dad while we were living with you!" I exclaimed.

"Okay. Well, once everything settles down, I'll move to Iowa, too."

I didn't know what to believe. *God, it's your will, not mine. Be my hands, feet, and mouth. Guard my heart and tongue.*

Journal Entry

Finally, Scott spoke to a lawyer. "Ruthless" is what Scott claims his lawyer said about the paperwork. Wasn't it ruthless the way Scott treated us? I'm completely at fault for protecting him all these years. For hiding the truth, making excuses, not pressing charges. I now fear I won't be able to protect the kids. Now Scott claims through text that he is changing: "God is bigger than this. Can't you give me another chance?"

I know God has the power to change him, but has he changed? God would want him to change and has already healed Scott and made all things new—but has Scott received the healing? Will Scott allow the change and rebuke any demonic powers that stand in his way? Scott can recite everything that John says, but that doesn't mean Scott has changed. He can talk the talk, but actions always speak louder than words.

I know I have to give Scott opportunities to prove his supposed change, so that is why Scott will get to continue to see the kids even if the kids don't like it. He wants supervised visits for only a period of time, which I understand.

Scott's changing is a journey, not a destination. He will have to work on it daily. So I'm supposed to let him be unsupervised, potentially place the kids in harm's way, and let abuse happen? Then I can press charges and file complaints after the fact? How is that in the best interest of the kids?

You are bigger than this, Lord. Protect my kids. They are getting older, so they can accurately report what is going on during these visits. Help me discern which way to go.

March 8, 2015

We went to church in the morning. Again I was filled with anxiety, knowing we would have to see Scott. He would be taking the kids for the afternoon at the Enners', and I was looking forward to a little me time.

As we left church, Ethan was obnoxious, saying rude things and making weird noises. When we got home, all three kids were out of sorts. At lunch Ethan threw rice across the kitchen.

"Ethan, clean up the rice you threw," I instructed.

Ethan threw himself on the floor in a tantrum, screaming, "I DIDN'T THROW THE RICE."

With his help, I eased him up off the floor, holding onto his upper arm. Ethan was kicking and screaming so much that Harley got scared and nipped Ethan's hand, which in turn made Ethan scream even more. I left Ethan on the floor to throw his tantrum. I didn't understand why Ethan acted like this. He was nine, not two.

Once he calmed down, Ethan proceeded to accuse me, "YOU ARE ABUSING ME, LIKE SCOTT!"

I was surprised that he had made that accusation. Immediately I felt bad, but I knew I had done nothing wrong.

"Oh Ethan, no, I'm not. You can't be throwing rice and not expect to clean it up," I pointed out.

He wanted to argue with me, but I ignored him and walked away. I supposed he was going to try this technique of saying that I was abusing him to get rid of me, too. *Good luck, kid; you're stuck with me.*

Ethan got more rambunctious, unable to control his body. He went into the living room where Kayla was and started making humping gestures in front of her body. Luckily, he didn't physically hump her.

"Ethan! That's inappropriate! STOP!" I yelled. We would need to keep working on this with his counselor.

"I don't want to see Scott anymore. I'm worried that Scott and you are going to get back together again. I don't want to go to the Enners' this afternoon," Erica pleaded.

"No, Erica, Scott and I are not going to get back together. The four of us are going to start over again, without Scott."

"Yeah, but I don't trust Scott. He implies too much. I don't want to go either."

"I understand. Scott is expecting all of you this afternoon, though. So everyone is going."

The truth was that I needed the break. A little peace and calm from this afternoon of acting out would be therapeutic for me.

The kids came home after their visit and enlightened me on all the information they had received from Scott.

"Scott talked to me about Ethan's humping," Kayla said. "Now I know Abigail's brother assaulted her and Stacy's brother assaulted her. It's haunting me now. What if Ethan does that?"

WHY WOULD HE HAVE TOLD HER THAT!

"No, Kayla, Ethan won't do that," I tried to console her. "We are going to keep seeing counselors."

Scott had disclosed way too much information about the biological family having a history of sexually assaulting each other. I wished Scott wouldn't have shared that detail.

While everyone was getting ready for bed, Ethan told me about his conversation with Scott. We were in his bedroom setting out clothes for the next day.

"Scott talked to me about body parts and what isn't appropriate," Ethan said.

"Oh, did you learn anything?" I asked.

"NOPE," Ethan responded matter-of-factly. "I was really uncomfortable. He started talking to me about sex and things that I didn't want to hear."

"Oh," I replied as noncommittally as possible.

The girls had said the same thing when I talked to them their bodies and sex, so I wasn't too caught off guard with what Ethan was saying.

"Scott flicked me in the head with his finger at dinner, too! It hurt!" Ethan complained.

"I saw it," Erica seconded, suddenly appearing in the bedroom door. "I don't think it was a big deal."

"What?!" Ethan countered. "It IS a big deal."

"You got flicked in the head because you were being rude at dinner again," Erica replied. I just let it slide. I didn't know what had happened or whether the Enners had been present; if they had been and didn't think much of it, then it was fine. Maybe Ethan was trying to get Scott into trouble.

March 13, 2015

The kids were going to see Scott's family over the weekend without Scott. I took them down and visited for a little bit with Sharon and Megan before I left for my parents'. It was a nice winter day, so the kids went outside to play.

I was still close with his family, and this life change was hard in terms of my relationships with them. I had always really enjoyed Scott's mom, Sharon, and would miss his sister-in-law, Megan, the most. We had become close friends.

"I will always be your friend, Heather," Megan assured me. "I can't believe how bad Scott screwed this up. I care about you and the kids."

"Thanks, Megan," I replied. "You're a great friend! Plus we might be able to move back so we can see each other more."

"That'd be awesome," Megan enthused.

Megan is a strong woman. Scott and she have never really gotten along.

"This wasn't a quick decision," I explained to them about the divorce. "The kids haven't attached to Scott emotionally. I'm not even sure they are attaching to me. However, Scott's behavior is detrimental to their emotional growth. I feel that Scott doesn't understand that, and he isn't going to change."

When it came time for me to leave, Ethen threw himself on the floor like a two-year-old and wanted to negotiate.

"You are okay, Ethan," I said to him. "I love you and will see you tomorrow." I left quickly.

I drove to my parents' house and enjoyed an evening there.

Scott texted me, "Hey, did you spend the $200 in cash I gave you last week for your dresses? You always look so nice in them. It would be good to have them altered, being you've lost so much weight."

"NO, it is stupid to spend money to have dresses altered. We have more important things to spend money on," I replied back through text.

Scott texted back, "It isn't stupid! I'll spend more money to provide for my family."

I chose not to respond. Was he trying to buy me? So much for a completely peaceful night at my parents'.

CHAPTER 30

Scott's Proposal

March 17, 2015

Scott retained a lawyer and responded to my proposal. He was fighting me over little things. I wished he would be willing to provide for his family by not dragging this out, costing us both more money and preventing his family from moving out of limbo. That was how he could provide—not by dress alterations.

Journal Entry

A part of me will always love Scott, care for him, and wish the best for him. However, not the "in love" part. The part that trusts, unconditionally loves, and would die for him, the way the wife should love her husband; that part has died. It's more a friend relationship now. Not many people have completely lost all my trust. A few. I don't know if I will ever be able to completely trust Scott again. I already had a broken, beat-up heart when I met him. I gave Scott all the pieces to it, trusting that he would help me put it back together.

I believe that if Scott would just have stayed by my side, not belittling me, and had let me heal myself it might have been better. I didn't want him or anyone but God to heal me.

"It's bad enough that I have to deal with what Chris did to you," Scott would often say to me.

I just wanted someone to love and support me while God and I worked on my heart. Now I'm getting my heart back in even more pieces than what I gave to Scott. I am afraid to give my heart to anyone else. I fear there may be nothing left.

I wish I knew when we get to move on with life. I want to get resettled, out of this house with terrible memories and into a new life, a fresh start. And seeking professional help for myself.

March 18, 2015

We saw Scott that evening at church, where he tried to give me a hug in front of everyone in the narthex.

"NO," I said firmly.

Scott leaned over and whispered in my ear, "The papers are not the truth; it's not what I really want. I was rushed and only had a short time to respond to the paperwork."

"You had weeks to take a look and decide what you want." I could feel my heartbeat getting quicker.

"I didn't understand what I was looking at." *He's smart and manipulative.* "I only had an hour for my consultation."

He'd had more time than that!

"What do you want, then?" I asked him.

"For it to be fair," Scott replied with a sly smile.

"No—what do you specifically want?" I replied, starting to get more aggravated.

"For it to be fair," Scott repeated with the same look on his face. UGH! Lies! He wanted me to create a scene in front of all our church parishioners!

"You are just wasting money, and it's stupid that you want me to alter dresses when we have lawyer fees and moving expenses," I responded in a low voice so as not to startle anyone, even though I wanted to scream at him.

"I'll give you more money! My lawyer is paid," Scott boasted back.

"Yeah, then they'll need more money because you'll waste it all not saying specifically what you want!" Despite myself, my voice raised a little. *Scott was just wasting time and money, hoping I'd give up and not move forward with the divorce.*

"I'm going as quickly as I can," Scott replied with attitude.

"I don't believe that for a second." With that I turned on my heel and left with the kids. As we walked away he called out, "Well, that's your opinion!"

At first talking to him I was extremely disappointed, suspecting that his lawyer was playing him for more money. Then, as he kept talking, digging his hole, I began getting truly angry. By the time we got home, however, I was calm again.

Journal Entry

Looking back at why I was angry, it's not because we are not done with this process. I know that God is in control of what is happening. It's because Scott was lying and trying to manipulate me again. Crap like "the paperwork isn't true," and "I was rushed," and "I just want it to be fair."

What the paperwork says is what he wants, to keep this going as long as possible. He will make up elaborate crap so that I don't sign, and that will drag this out. So I'll have to figure out what is most important to me—MOVING—and find the lesser of the evils when it comes to money.

We will probably have to go to mediation. Hopefully we can move by the time school gets out in May because I will need a job. I hate to start a new job in Omaha for the summer to have to quit by fall. Yet Scott tells the kids that he hopes I don't sign the papers. Then he tells them HE hopes to move to Iowa by fall. So it sounds as though he is still letting us move. I hope.

I'll just have to wait and see. God, I know you are in control. Please give the kids and me peace as we wait in hope for this to be over soon. I just want to move on.

March 30, 2015

Lately I had been at peace. Then I would have my moments of doubt, thinking that maybe Scott had indeed changed. Pastor Danica and John Enner both reported that they could see changes. The kids admitted that they, too, could see some changes by then as well. Kayla reflected, however, "Something isn't quite right, but I can't figure it out."

The other day we had met with Pastor Danica to go over the divorce paperwork. She had been our mediator and had been helping us get things lined up for our lawyers. As we were going through some money-related issues, Scott said to me in front of Pastor Danica, "It's not about the money like it used to be. Heather, you are such a wonderful person. I really messed things up and I blame myself daily."

When Pastor Danica left the room for a moment, Scott commented, "I make 70% of the income, and I will have to pay 70% of unreimbursed medical bills, so I should get 70% of the tax return."

I couldn't respond. I'm sure a look of surprise was all over my face. Surprise not that I wanted the money or that this was what I cared about. No, I was surprised by the fact that he had just beforehand said it was not about money, about how he had changed, . . . but immediately afterward acted differently behind Pastor Danica's back.

I left our meeting very distraught.

CHAPTER 31

April Drama

April 2, 2015

A couple of days later, Scott asked to go to the house once the kids were in school and I went to work. He claimed that he needed more clothes. I had already moved everything valuable to me to my friend's house.

"Where are the guns?" Scott asked me a little later via text.

My heart rate increased. Why would he be in the basement if he were looking for clothes? I held my ground: "They are in a safe place, and you will get them back eventually."

"WHERE ARE THEY?" He put his text in all caps.

"They are safe," I repeated.

"Well, you missed one. I had one in the closet and I've grabbed it."

I kind of remembered him having one there but hadn't seen it recently. Now I was debating what to do. Was this a threat or just information?

I talked to a coworker who was an ex-cop. He took a look at the texts.

"You may want to look into a restraining order, being that he grabbed a gun from the closet. The police won't do anything now, though, about his having a gun."

I didn't know what to do. I felt as though I wanted to have this conversation documented. I really didn't think Scott had it in him to hurt me. I decided just to let it slide.

April 3, 2015

It was Easter weekend, and Scott would be seeing the kids in Osceola with his family. Russell was going to supervise over the weekend. The kids and I went to Iowa, where I had Russell meet me to exchange the kids because I didn't care to see Scott. Scott texted me while I was at my parents' house.

"Don't make a habit out of Russell meeting you in town without me. It takes away from my parenting time."

Yeah, the whole ten minutes it takes Russell to get the kids back to Scott at the farm. It's not that it takes away from his parenting time. It's the fact that he isn't seeing me to push his control on me. I want to see as little of Scott as possible. That's what a divorce is: separate lives.

"Fine, but in the future when you drop off and pick up the kids at my future house, you will not be allowed in," I texted back.

"I have a right to see inside the house and the kids' living establishment."

"WRONG!"

My blood was boiling by then. Not going to happen. That would be the kids' safe haven. Their only security from him and the world. I chose not to read or respond to his last text and stormed around my parents' house while I fumed.

After the weekend I was tucking Ethan into bed.

"Scott and I never talk when we're together. I was with Russell a lot during the weekend. Russell does fun things with me."

By the way the kids were talking, Scott seemed to be avoiding Ethan and concentrating just on the girls. He had even sent Ethan away recently to go play on a Wednesday night at church. I needed to find Ethan a good male role model. We needed to get out of Omaha.

"Until now you have not asked for anything in my name. Ask and you will receive, and your joy will be complete" (John 16:24).

April 7, 2015

God blessed us with a house to rent in Leon! It was the first house I had looked at a few months earlier, and I absolutely loved it. It has four bedrooms and plenty of room. At the time the landlord wasn't going to take Harley, but now he was willing, as long as I provided a down payment! I even had the option of buying this house in the future.

I knew God would provide a good job next. With each day I was more encouraged that I was doing the right thing. I was realizing just how controlling Scott actually was and recognizing that I was not the crazy one. I still wished the best for Scott, but my first priority was getting away from him.

April 8, 2015

We had church that evening. I dreaded going to church. We went twice a week and had to see Scott each time.

I had found out the day before about the attempted suicide of Becky, Scott's niece. It was a cry for help. I felt for her. I knew she was blue and hoped she would get the help she needed.

"I still don't have paperwork done due to Becky's circumstance and having to babysit the Enner kids," Scott claimed after I had questioned him about how it was coming.

"You need to get your priorities straight. Your own kids should be coming before all other kids. I know Becky's situation is upsetting, but there is nothing for you to do three hours away."

"Oh, you know about Becky? What do you know? Her situation is bad. I just don't know what to do about it," Scott said in a rush.

He was playing games—trying to make a big deal of Becky's incident, not knowing how much I knew about it.

"I would appreciate the paperwork in one week to get your own kids out of limbo." With that I turned and walked away.

I believed that Scott was dragging his feet. I was really calm. I was finally seeing his true colors: it was still all about him and what he could get out of the situation. I was not sure what I could do to speed Scott up.

John Enner's expressions lately had been bothersome to me. He looked exhausted or sad. I hoped that Scott wasn't wearing down the Enner family. Maybe I should text John's wife that I was thinking of them. I was sure Scott couldn't keep the charade going forever. It had been a little over two months—the longest Scott's act had ever lasted.

These thoughts of mine are not Christian. Please, God, give me your eyes. I do see Scott's good side, but I sure see the evil side, too. Judgment is the Lord's prerogative, not mine. I pray that Scott gets his priorities straight soon, though, so we can all move forward.

CHAPTER 32

May Drama

May 8, 2015

A whole month, and still no lawyer communication. As school was drawing closer to an end, I was almost in a panic, with my job ending soon. Scott was still evasive about whether he would permit us to move to Iowa in the near future. The kids were also acting up, aware of the possibility of limbo in the near future.

Over a week earlier Ethan had pinned Kayla in a corner, threatening to kill her. I didn't see it, but Kayla seemed pretty shook up about it. Ethan brushed it off, as though he had been kidding and nothing had really happened. I didn't know what to believe.

Erica had a slumber party at her friend's house. The girls decided in the middle of the night that it would be a good idea to go outside and look at the stars. They wanted a good view, so they lay in the street! Of course, there were boys involved.

Neighbors were concerned about children lying in the street in the middle of the night, so the police were called and ended up calling the parents. Needless to say, that ended the overnight. I picked her up and brought her home. Who knew what had really happened? But that was the story she was sticking to. Oh boy—almost fourteen. The stupidity was starting.

The owner of our house knew about our situation by this time. She wanted to sell the house as quickly as possible and get rid of our quick claim deed agreement. That meant that we would be out of a house in Omaha soon.

Hopefully we would get to move to Iowa the following weekend! Scott claimed that we could go but refused to sign any paperwork stating that outright. He also refused to get on his lawyers' case to hurry up the process.

Journal Entry

Come, Lord Jesus, I hate this world. I realize why I like to sleep. It's the closest thing to the spiritual world. It is so hard relying on you when I can't see where we are going. I know that's where the faith part comes in. Trust the Lord, not man. You cannot trust the human, unpredictable, selfish creatures we are.

May 10, 2015

The day prior we had met with Pastor Danica again. Scott was all Dr. Jeckyl in front of Pastor Danica: "Take whatever you want in belongings. I have been unfair for years," he said in apparent generosity. "I'll take care of the house situation."

Then during the course of our conversation in the parking lot I saw My Hyde: "The contract says I don't have to pay the owner anything," and "I want the kitchen table and dishes."

"I don't care about any of the material things. I just want you to make up your mind."

The next day at church he had to save face in front of everyone.

"I was right the first time. It's whatever the kids need, so take what they need because by the time they are ready to visit me and my house I can have things bought again."

Ethan's psychiatrist had recently told us that seeing Scott was detrimental to Ethan's wellbeing at this time. Scott seemed to understand and respect this. He wanted to have the girls spend the night at the Enners' that evening with him. The girls were nervous about this. I was supporting them with whatever decision they might make.

At church Scott told Erica, "Ethan isn't going this evening because Ethan is so uncomfortable around me."

That got Erica thinking. She had by this point decided that she wasn't comfortable around Scott, either.

"Well, we have to give Scott a chance," Kayla announced to her siblings.

Which was truthful. How much do you trust someone after they have hurt you over and over again? It sounded as though Kayla was still going to the Enners', but the day was young.

The girls decided not to spend the night with Scott, but they did go shopping with him that afternoon. Scott helped the girls shop for Mother's Day gifts and bought them whatever they wanted.

"It's like he's trying to buy us. That's good for you, Mom—less money you need to spend!" Kayla remarked. That was not an ethic I wanted to instill in her.

The girls claimed that Scott had told them again that he was unsure whether we would get to move to Iowa. This caused them high anxiety about the unknown—about the uncertainty of where we would be living in one short week.

Scott came into the house while he dropped the girls back off. "I won't go to the courthouse to file the quick claim deed because I don't want to take off work."

"Fine," I told him, "I'll print off the deed and meet you at the bank on your lunch break tomorrow to have it notarized. I'll take it to the courthouse myself."

Scott frustrated me so. "Can you sign this paper that I wrote up stating that you are allowing us to move?" I asked him while he stood in the doorway to our house.

"You can move. My lawyer says I don't have to sign anything."

The signing was for my own peace of mind. Scott continued, "I won't charge you with kidnapping. What would I gain? If I really wanted you to stay, I would say no."

I still didn't trust him and had a small, nagging doubt.

"Please stop telling the kids we are getting back together," I told him, as I thought about what the kids had told me earlier.

"You don't know what the future holds."

No, I don't, but it looks less likely every day for us to get back together, I thought to myself.

Every day he was showing me more and more clearly how ill he really is. I'm hearing from so many people all the bridges he has burned and the hurt he has inflicted. Yet he invariably plays the victim.

So with that, we were getting ready to move! Packing and boxing things up. Getting a U-Haul lined up. Scott was going to keep his stuff in the house even after we left. He stated that he would take care of everything related to the house. I believed I would end up, one way or another, getting screwed.

The next day we signed the quitclaim deed for the house. Scott barely said two words to me at the bank.

Journal Entry

My emotions are running high. I'm keeping my Bible close. I have mixed emotions. Happy for a new start, a new life, a new me. But sad about closing a chapter and a failed marriage. I failed. I gave up. Did I give up too early? I hope and pray for Scott daily that this will make him rely on God, relinquish control, and truly become closer to our Lord and let Him mold him into the man God wants him to be. Scott has hurt and upset a lot of people. I pray that he sees what has happened, is reconciled, and forgives himself and asks for forgiveness.

I pray that the kids and I can one day trust him again. I believe I have forgiven him because I wish him no harm—all the best, in fact, even when he is at his worst. I wish he would turn fully to God instead of listening to all those other voices.

I don't think I can ever trust Scott again, though. I know all about turning the other cheek, forgiving seven times seventy-seven, but the Bible also says to trust only in God. I know that one day He will give me an answer. Thank you, God, for Jesus and His ultimate sacrifice for me and for all.

May 12, 2015

The dissolution response came two months later—but hey, things were moving again. It actually looked signable, so I made an appointment on that Friday with my lawyer. I was getting screwed financially, but money didn't mean much to me. I would get to have the kids and Harley and to move to Iowa.

I would find a way. Actually, God would. I was thankful not to be tied to Scott financially any longer. I knew that Scott would provide for the kids financially because that was all he knew how to do. He didn't understand how to support them emotionally or spiritually. Scott also didn't know how to make amends or offer comfort, but he could make the kids comfortable with material things.

Journal Entry

I'm still going to try to pray for Scott every day. In God's eyes we are still married. Other people keep saying that I'm young and can move on and even have more kids. Do I really want to? I'm very unsure what God would say about that. In God's Word I would be an adulteress to the next man, and he would be condemned. No, I can't have another man ever. Plus, I don't need another child, even though it has been weighing on me that I'm going to have a baby around the month of March.

If I do find another man, I will need him to be a strong follower of God. Walk the walk, not just talk the talk. He will have to be patient, kind, comforting, and someone who can listen to me and not try to fix me. Just be by my side through life, helping us grow closer to God. He has to put God before me. This guy does not exist. He would have to be Jesus.

Scott is incapable of any of that. He can't put God first. I know that's a hard test for me too, but I have yet to see Scott do it. Even before thinking of dating again, this new guy would have to impress my kids, be a good role model for Ethan, and be supportive. :) Smile.

CHAPTER 33

Our New Beginning

May 27, 2015

We moved to Leon, Iowa! My family and extended family were a huge help! Everyone chipped in to help with moving vehicles and the U-Haul. Even Megan and Kelly came to help once we got to Iowa. The kids were excited! Everything ran smoothly, and I couldn't have asked for a better day.

We settled into our new house and a new routine. I got on food assistance to help feed the circus. The kids explored the town on their bikes and found some local parks, including the pool. I went to the park and rec office and purchased pool passes for the summer. I had about a month's cushion before I had to find a job.

Within a week I had an interview with the local hospital. I received a job offer at the local daycare, but it was at minimum wage. That wouldn't get us by. I accepted the job but was waiting for a month to start to give me a chance to get settled and possibly hear back from the hospital.

For the time being, it was decided that every other weekend Scott would be coming from Omaha, Nebraska, to Osceola, Iowa, to see the kids with supervision. Ethan would be included back on those visits. Scott hadn't liked that Ethan was missing out and agreed to be supervised by his family and various other people here in Iowa whom we both trusted. He would need to be supervised for a year, and then we would re-evaluate the situation with a mediator.

The kids and Scott also needed to attend reunification sessions, where they would meet with a qualified therapist and try to mend their relationship. We had made progress on our dissolution but still hadn't reached an agreement. Scott was dragging his feet.

We attended a local church, finding the people friendly and likeable. I met Amy from the local hotel there, and she offered me a job at her front registration desk. I preferred that opportunity to the daycare.

I was supposed to hear something on a particular day from the hospital but had not heard yet and was starting to believe I hadn't gotten the hospital job. That would be okay. God would provide. I planned to call Amy later on in the week if I didn't hear anything from the hospital.

I hadn't heard much from Scott but knew that he had received the latest round of divorce papers. I needed the child support to be fair but was not overly worried at that time.

We had met Carol, Ethan's counselor, for the first time. I chose Carol because she is knowledgeable about PTSD and RAD. Unfortunately, she was located in the next town over, so there would be some extra running. Ethan seemed to connect with her, and I was hopeful.

I also got the girls started with Brenda, their shared counselor. She would be able to pick them up right from the school once school started, meeting with them when they had some downtime in the school day. This would eliminate some unnecessary running for me.

Many changes, and meeting lots of people. I now needed to find a counselor for myself. There wasn't a large pool from which to choose in rural Iowa. I was dealing with a lot of raw emotion, and little triggers would upset me. I wanted to go back to being carefree and to deal in particular with my OCD. I felt as though some of Scott's bad habits had rubbed off on me. I needed to deflect Ethan's temper tantrums, avoid absorbing his negative energy, and stop engaging in his arguments. I needed to become more aware. Tomorrow would be a new day.

Journal Entry

Thank you, God, for your sacrifice of Jesus to save my life. Let me try again and again, even though I don't deserve it. I am so blessed. I pray that everyone I know and love finds you, trusts, and relies in you.

May 28, 2015

My parents came to visit, and we went to the local pool. We sat outside the pool while the kids played.

"Collin came to the farm to survey our land," my dad commented. *Collin was the kids' adult cousin who had helped his parents take care of them for eight months.* "He usually doesn't do our county but was filling in for someone," Dad continued. "I didn't realize who he was at first, until we started talking more."

"Oh, that's funny!" I replied. "What a small world."

"At the end of the visit Collin said to say hi to you and Scott," Dad went on. "That made me realize that you hadn't told the kids' family that you were back yet, so I said nothing about the separation."

I didn't know whether I wanted to tell the biological family that we were back for fear of the biological mom and dad finding out and hunting us down. That was my biggest fear. I guessed my worst underlying fear was somehow losing the kids. That they wouldn't want to be with me anymore, and I would fail to get them on the right path.

"You should probably let them know," my mom advised. "The kids always really liked Kenneth and Marie."

June 1, 2016

I decided that Kenneth, Marie, and Collin would be okay. I knew that the kids' family would eventually find out anyway. I had to start trusting people somewhere along the way. I contacted Marie through email:

"I wanted to let you know that Scott and I are going through a divorce. The kids and I have moved back to the area. We now live in Leon. The kids have always loved you guys, so we hope to keep in touch. Please don't tell Abigail if you happen to talk to her. I don't need the drama yet from that side of the family."

Marie emailed me back by the end of the day:

"I'm sorry to hear that you are going through a divorce. That must be hard on the kids and you. Collin is now working in Leon. He still lives in Osceola but makes the commute to Leon. I'm sure he would be more than willing to come over when he gets off work and help in any way that he can." Marie gave me Collin's phone number.

What luck! Collin would be a great role model for Ethan, and he could pick him up and take him hunting and fishing again, just as he used to. I contacted Collin via text: *"Hi Collin, this is Heather. I talked to your mom through email and she gave me your phone number."*

I pushed send and waited for a reply. I diddled around the house, picking up dishes and starting laundry.

After some time Collin responded back: *"Hi Heather, how's it going?"*

"I wanted to let you know that the kids and I moved to Leon, so we are back in the area. Scott and I are getting a divorce. After talking to your mom she said that you work in Leon. I was wondering if you'd like to set something up for you and Ethan to get together to go fishing."

"Oh, I am sorry to hear that," Collin replied. *"Yes, I would love to hang with Ethan and take him out. What works for you?"*

We decided that the following week would work best for all. Ethan would be excited!

Journal Entry

I received the job at the hospital today! God is good. I am happy I decided to be patient and not get over excited. I knew God would come through. I'm sorry I doubted.

CHAPTER 34

June Drama

June 8, 2015

It had been a rough week with the kids—terrible, actually. Mouthy, rude, defiant. I was sure this was all about the unknown future and not having much of a schedule. I told them that we would be meeting with Collin on Wednesday and that if they wanted to go they needed to start helping out and making better choices. They were excited! Over the next couple of days things seemed to have returned to normal.

Ethan was still erupting in rages during which he seemed unable to control his body. I talked with Carol about his outbursts.

"No more contact with Scott until further notice. He has PTSD from Scott. Seeing Scott, even the thought of seeing Scott, triggers him. We can't let Ethan keep getting triggered until he is healed."

Scott had been quiet lately in terms of demands, and I wasn't sure how he would take this news again.

I informed through text: "*Carol is Ethan's counselor. She said that Ethan shouldn't see you until further notice again due to his PTSD. We need to heal Ethan so that the triggers stop.*"

He answered almost immediately: "*I want to talk to Ethan on the phone then. I want to hear it from him that he doesn't want to see me.*"

"*I'll have to ask Carol.*" I wasn't sure whether phone contact in itself would trigger Ethan or whether Scott would manipulate him.

I was in the living room and had just finished my text conversation with Scott when I got an uneasy feeling in my stomach. The same one that had always told me something was going on with the kids. Kayla was in the kitchen being eerily quiet. I went into the kitchen and saw her back to me by the front door. The key holder that hangs on the wall fell at her feet.

She turned around and looked at me in surprise that I had come into the kitchen.

"What are you doing?" I asked her.

"Nothing—this just fell on the floor," Kayla replied, picking up the key holder.

By the looks of the key holder it had been taken apart, piece by piece. The small hanging apples were now mangled, twisted, and pulled apart.

"What happened to it, Kayla?" I asked.

"I just told you, it fell on the floor," she replied coldly.

I knew she was lying to me. Kayla has been on a kick lately of destroying her things or getting rid of stuff. I decided that I needed to address this destruction with her counselor, too. At least Erica appeared to be doing well with our transition back to Iowa, . . . unless I was missing something.

Journal Entry: June 10, 2015

The kids met with Collin today. They were all a chatter when they saw him. They hung from him like monkeys on a monkey bar, all trying to get his attention. I watched and wished Scott could have been like that.

They need a good role model. I'm thankful Collin works in town and wants to spend time with them. They are missing a father figure. I wish I could wipe away all their pain. I wish Scott could have loved them. I wish we could have worked out. I was so blinded by Scott. I never really saw the true Scott.

I tried, I think, to make this work. Was it enough? Why am I not good enough? I must not be relying on God enough. God is testing me, and I keep failing. God, you are amazing. You have given me so much: kids, Harley, awesome house, job, car, family, an awesome support system, strength, courage, Faith; they all come from you.

Do not harden your heart like a rock. A rock erodes on the outside, but nothing changes inside. Instead, be a sponge in the ocean, soaking up God and all that is around you. "I can do all this through Him who gives me strength" (Philippians 4:13).

June 15, 2015

A week later Collin came over while my parents were visiting. Ethan and Collin started throwing the football around in the yard. *That was something Scott had never done.*

As I watched them play I was talking to my parents, but absentmindedly. I was watching Collin's hands. They are big and strong, yet gentle. Safe. I shook myself out of my daze. *NO. Not going down that road. No.*

Collin and Ethan continued to play. After a while it was time for Collin to get going back home to Osceola. He had just stopped by after work to say hello. Ethan hated seeing him go. I felt good knowing that Collin was going to be a good role model for him. After Collin left my mom teased me: "Collin would be a fine man to start dating . . ."

"WHAT?! No. I'm not ready for that," I replied.

June 18, 2015

Scott's weekend was coming up. Ethan was not going this time—the first weekend since Carol had said no. Scott had never addressed the issue again of wanting to talk to Ethan on the phone. As the weekend drew near, the girls were getting anxious about their visit with Scott.

They brought up some issues that had been bothering them. I was starting to worry about our arrangements already. Being that it was summer, they were spending most of their time inside the camper at Scott's family farm.

I decided to compose an email to Scott to address the girls' issues:

"As the weekend is drawing closer the girls' anxiety is starting to peak, and they have mentioned a few things that they are worried about it, and quite frankly so am I. If this arrangement is to continue, here are a few boundaries that you will have to abide by:

1. *Becky is not 18 yet. She is not an acceptable supervisor.*
2. *The girls will no longer change bras or any other clothing in front of you. Covering your eyes while they change is unacceptable. They need to find a different room in the camper to change, or you step outside. They are now young women, not little girls.*
3. *The girls will no longer sleep with you, and you will not ask them to.*
4. *I want your supervised visit reports that are stated in the divorce decree to start immediately. I know Pastor Danica created a good outline that you should have a copy of yet, or you could ask her to create it again."*

It took only an hour or so for Scott to respond:

"Well, I can tell the girls didn't tell you the whole story, or told you what you wanted to hear.

1. *Yes, Becky is not 18, and I will not do it again until she is.*

2. *You're right the girls are becoming young women, so after a movie Kayla forgot to take off her bra. I gave her choices: 1. Get out of bed and go change. 2. Sleep with it on. 3. I bury myself with the comforter WITH HER LEG OVER ME. Kayla made her own choice. If she was uncomfortable then she wouldn't have made the choice she did.*

3. *The first night it was really hot in the camper, and Erica was saying it was too hot in the top bunk and she could not sleep. So I gave her options: 1. Move to the other bottom bunk. 2. Sleep on the floor. 3 Move up to the table with me. I left her to decide. A minute or two later she had made her choice. The next night we were watching a movie, Erica got up and went to bed when she got tired. Kayla decided to stay where she was when the movie was over. I did not ask her to stay. The girls are young women, and I know that. I'm their dad, not a stranger or a sex offender. As young women, I am giving them different options, and they make their own choices.*

4. *Sorry the last report was not very neat, but I will have a form created for the next time."*

Disturbing, yet no one would listen. Scott was causing me so much anxiety. I would bring this to my lawyer.

CHAPTER 35

Canoeing and Dinner

June 20, 2015

Ethan and I went on a canoe trip with Collin and a couple of my friends. My friends were staying at a campground in Osceola and invited Ethan and me to join them. I invited Collin over because Ethan loved hanging out with him.

Getting Ethan down from his excitement about Collin's coming along was a challenge. Collin and he fished a lot, so Ethan was ecstatic and wanted to bring his fishing pole along the river with him while he canoed.

I was very new to this and didn't want to deal with the logistics. However, Collin said,

"Oh, Ethan knows what he is doing. I've been teaching him since he was four. Plus, I'll help Ethan take care of it."

I was able to let go and rely on someone else to take care of Ethan! With Scott I always worried and felt like I needed to supervise every exchange.

After canoeing, Collin and I sat in the grass at the campground while Ethan ran around playing with other kids. My friends did their own thing, and Collin and I had a good visit. I told him about all the things that had been going on.

"I had no idea," Collin replied. "You all seemed so happy when I saw you. The last time I saw you was at Kayla's birthday party."

"That was the time I was so nervous because I wasn't sure Scott could keep it together. We were falling apart as a family."

"You all put up a really good act."

I laughed: "Yeah, the act started to become second nature for me."

"It's strange that I ended up at your parents' farm," Collin reflected. "I normally don't work that county, but I was filling in for someone else. I told your dad to tell you and Scott hi, and there was a confused look on your dad's face. I figured maybe he didn't understand what I said."

"Dad told me about that. He said that's when he figured out that you didn't know yet about the divorce," I replied. "I agree—it is weird that you ended up at my parents'. It's really weird how the kids and I ended up in Leon, too."

"Oh, yeah, how did you end up there?"

"I basically looked at a map online. I looked for something close to my parents but not too close for the biological parents. I wanted something that I could easily commute from if needed for a job but that had a decent school district. I don't know why, but I kept leaning toward Leon."

"That's interesting."

I then started thinking about what it was that had actually drawn me to Leon. There had been something about Leon that I couldn't quite figure out, as though God were telling me to go there. I now had a job there that I loved. I couldn't help but think now that maybe it was because Collin worked there. He lived in Osceola but made the commute every day to Leon for work. This was the perfect opportunity for Ethan to have an excellent role model.

We talked for a while longer about each other's jobs and his hunting and fishing excursions with Ethan. Collin talked about bow hunting and how he eventually wanted to take Ethan bow hunting once he was old enough. I got excited about this because I had recently started archery myself.

"Maybe you can help me set up my bow," I suggested.

"I don't know much about compound bows, being I use a cross bow."

"Oh! I forgot you had your heart valve replaced a year ago!"

Collin had been born with a heart condition and was on his second heart valve replacement. Kenneth and Marie had mentioned that on one of our visits with the kids.

We had dinner with my friends, after which we headed our separate ways. Collin and I left it that we would be in touch soon for another adventure with Ethan and the girls.

July 7, 2015

Ethan's attitude fluctuated daily, but he was coming around to following directions and not acting out as much. The girls' pattern was one of doing okay until they saw Scott, after which we would go through a few days of attitude.

Collin and I were starting to hang out more and more, as friends, with the kids. The kids loved interacting with Collin. We went out to eat, fish, and canoe together. We all laughed and joked around and "picked" on each other.

We went out to eat one evening at the local Chinese restaurant. The kids were a chatter about their day.

The landlord had come over that day to fix my bedroom window.

"I led him up to Heather's room," Ethan explained. "There on her bed was her thong!"

My face must have changed every shade of red, and I could feel my cheeks warm. "ETHAN!" I exclaimed.

The girls burst out into laughter, and Collin put his head down to hide his smile.

"It was a nightgown—at least get it right!" I teased back.

We all laughed, but I was still slightly embarrassed because it had been true. The landlord and Ethan had gotten an eyeful. Too bad I'd had no idea people were going to be in my room.

These kinds of exchanges would have been impossible to enjoy with Scott. Scott would always make things uncomfortable and had so many rules. I felt comfortable around Collin, as though I could tell him anything and he wouldn't judge me for it.

I started Ethan with a new psychiatrist whom Carol recommended. After visiting with him a couple of times and talking about Ethan's reactive attachment disorder, the psychiatrist started him on an antidepressant and a mood stabilizer. We finally found the right dosage for Ethan! It was enough that it did not sedate him. Plus, it was enough that Ethan was making well-thought-out decisions before acting out to destroy. Yay!

CHAPTER 36

Hanging Out Together

July 19, 2015

Collin and my little family continued to hang out as friends. The girls visited with Scott every other weekend, and Ethan stayed with me. The girls weren't overly excited to see Scott, yet they weren't complaining. Collin, Ethan, and I went on another canoeing trip that weekend, this time with a bunch of Collin's friends.

Ethan and I were in a canoe, and Collin took his own kayak. As we are going down the river, I noticed that one of Collin's friends was flirting with him. She was splashing water on him and trying to get her own kayak close to his to tip him over. I felt an overwhelming surge of jealousy flood over me.

What is that?! Collin is just a friend. That's all. You are not ready to date. It appeared that Collin wasn't reciprocating the flirting, though. He just paddled on and eventually met back up with Ethan and me.

As we continued to float down the river, we came across cattle in the water. This is a normal thing in this area, as this section of the river flows through pastureland. The river wasn't that high that weekend, and the cows were there getting drinks. However, they didn't like to move to accommodate passersby. There also happened to be slight rapids in this area. I was in the back of the canoe, steering the craft.

I told Ethan, "Put your paddle in so I can steer us out of the mess. Hang on—this could get ugly!"

To my surprise, Ethan listened and pulled his paddle in without complaint. Dodging cattle while following the rapids was a challenge, and I was thankful Ethan listened and didn't put his paddle back into the water to change our course.

We were the first ones through and made it with no problem. I turned around and watched the others. One by one, they each tipped over! Collin almost made it through, but right at the end he dumped his kayak.

Later Collin commented on how worried he had been about Ethan and me going through that mess. He showed genuine concern, although, I told myself, maybe it was just for Ethan.

Collin said, "That was impressive that you managed your way through without tipping over."

"What can I say—I'm a pro!" I teased.

"I guess I better take lessons from you, being as I tipped!" he teased back.

I eventually lost track of time. I was supposed to meet Scott at a specific time to pick up the girls. Kyle and Megan were supervisors for the weekend. The girls always enjoyed hanging out with them and their kids, Kelly and Ryker. They said they always felt safe with Megan. I felt good leaving them with her, too. We are still friends, even though I was going through a divorce with her brother-in-law.

Being that I was late, I was anxious, as usual. Also, given that Collin was a neighbor of Kyle and Megan, we would have to drive past their house to get to his. I didn't need Scott jumping to the conclusion that Collin and I were an item.

As we got closer to Collin's house, I got more and more nervous. Collin asked, "Are you okay? You don't look so good."

As we drove past Kyle and Megan's house they were all standing outside, looking very hostile. Megan and Scott were having an argument, facing each other swinging arms in the air as they argued. Everyone else stood there watching. The girls looked horrified.

We got to Collin's house, where Ethan decided to stay to avoid seeing Scott. I didn't want to see him, either! I walked down to Kyle and Megan's house. By now Scott had already left. The girls were gathering their stuff, and Megan was visibly upset. Megan and Scott never had gotten along. They didn't see eye-to-eye, having different perspectives on how things should be done. We had a discussion on what had happened, and the girls and I went on our way back to Collin's house.

"What did you do this weekend?" Kayla asked me on our walk up the hill.

"Ethan and I went canoeing with Collin," I replied.

"WHAT?! That's not fair! You guys get to do something fun with Collin, and we have to go with Scott!" she snapped back quickly.

She had a good point. It didn't sound as though they'd had a good weekend with Scott. Ethan and I, on the other hand, had enjoyed a great day with Collin.

"I'm sorry, Kayla," I said. "We'll try to do more fun things on the weekends you're with me."

Erica was quiet.

July 20, 2015

I composed an email to Scott based on the information I had received from the girls and Megan about the weekend and what had led to the argument in the driveway:

"Hello.

I have developed a schedule and requirements for weekends that you have the girls. I will have the girls to Osceola by 7 p.m. Friday nights. Usually they should be there before that, but if I run into a snag and I'm working until 6 the girls will be there by 7. I will continue to bring them to Kyle and Megan unless they decide to not be a part of this anymore, or if the weekend doesn't work for them. Then I will contact other members of your family to create an alternative plan. We will meet for exchange Sunday evenings at 6 p.m. at the gas station, diesel side. If this doesn't work we will contact each other and make alternative arrangements. You will be informed of things that pertain to your pick up and drop off. Other people or places that are irrelevant to you do not need to be disclosed.

Please divulge information to ALL of your family what your plans are, where you want to go, and who you would like to have supervise you for that outing prior to the weekend. You will follow their direction on sleeping arrangements without complaint.

You will no longer harass your family and bring them to tears, especially in front of the kids!

If this cannot be followed, please look into purchasing a supervised visitation provider and relieve your family from this responsibility."

As expected, there was no response back.

July 25, 2015

The kids and I went to Kenneth and Marie's for their annual get-together. It was Osceola days, and every year they have a get-together with their family and friends. This wasn't the same side of the family as the kids'. It was Marie's immediate family with whom we were getting together.

The kids were excited, as they knew everyone and reminisced about the days when they had lived with Kenneth, Marie, and Collin.

Kenneth and Marie invited us to stay overnight, and the kids were ecstatic! We brought Harley up with us, and he ran with Collin's dog, Odin. Collin's other dog, Savannah, had passed away the Christmas before. Our two dogs got along really well, considering that Odin was a puppy and Harley was older and didn't typically tolerate other dogs that well.

We enjoyed playing beanbags in their family tournament. Collin and I became increasingly flirty. We were on opposite teams, and we started shooting each other a lot of grief. He made me smile and laugh and was very funny and charming. The best part was that the kids love him! They already had such a great bond.

Between the two of us we started a game based on the controversy over which is stronger in terms of influence on kids, nature or nurture. If the kids said something funny or smart, we would banter back and forth about whether it was the product of nature or nurture. "Nature" would mean that this was just the way the kids were—some hereditary trait from Collin's extended family, perhaps. "Nurture" would apply to a behavior they had learned from me.

Ethan asked politely whether he could have a pop. "See, look at that nurture shining through!" I would tease Collin.

Kayla teased Ethan, making fun of his hair. "I'm seeing that nurturing," Collin remarked.

By the end of the night we were holding hands as we visited with his family in the dark by the campfire. The kids were inside, so I felt comfortable holding his hand. I'm not sure how it started. My hand just somehow ended up in his.

We didn't speak about our feelings to each other. I was really starting to wonder what I was supposed to do. I shouldn't have even been thinking about dating, but I was starting to feel like the biblical Ruth in her encounters with Boaz!

Journal Entry: August 2, 2015

We are still abundantly blessed, but I'm having a hard time with Scott. He has now changed the paperwork to fight for full custody! Ugh.

I am stronger now than ever. I started seeing a counselor, and she started me on an antidepressant. My counselor is helping me see my worth. I'm realizing that I have had anxiety and depression all my life. This is where my anxiousness and negative self-talk come from. Sounds like these are issues I will always have to work on, day in and day out.

She is also pointing out things that I had never seen before about Scott and our relationship and explaining to me why I didn't see these characteristics before. There is no shame in counseling. I am proud of myself for going. I wish I would have started this sooner. Maybe it would have given me strength a long time ago.

My counselor has also pointed out that Ethan and I both have PTSD from Scott. This is why we both have triggers and we each get triggered by the other. I associate Ethan with Scott by the way Ethan behaves. Ethan still likes to be in control and is always all about himself. When Ethan acts controlling it triggers me because it reminds me of Scott. This, too, is something I will have to continuously work on.

CHAPTER 37

Chanting and Abigail

August 3, 2015

Lately Kayla had been extremely angry with Scott. "I don't want to have a relationship with him!" she would often scream at me.

Over the course of the past couple of months—more noticeably since we had moved—Kayla had been grappling with a multitude of issues that seemed to be getting worse. She was becoming very angry over everything, especially chores and having to help out around the house. Kayla liked to destroy belongings, especially her own. She would scream at me and Ethan and say hateful things to us—especially me. Kayla would even put herself down, but she would put the words in our mouths, claiming we were saying these things about her.

Kayla had a very low sense self-worth and believed that she was fat and that no one liked her. She lied a lot about unimportant things and seemed to be paranoid.

Kayla kept telling me, "I don't need parents. I don't need you or Scott. I am not going to follow the rules because I DON'T NEED YOU" and "I want to eat when I want and have a refrigerator in my room."

Kayla used food as a coping mechanism. She ate when she was anxious or upset—which lately seemed to have been constantly. I tried to keep healthy food in the house, but it was expensive, so junk made it in.

To compound the problem, people here in Leon (who are abundantly nice) brought us cookies and treats all the time! It upset Erica and Ethan when Kayla continuously ate all the junk food. I tried to monitor her eating a little, and this made her more self-conscious.

"You think I'm fat! Stop calling me fat!" she would scream at me, even though I had never called her that.

At night we would all go into our separate bedrooms that are on the same floor. The girls were to have quiet time, and Ethan went to bed at about 8:00 p.m. Erica at fourteen put herself to bed, while Kayla, still eleven, needed a little guidance to maintain a sleep schedule. I would have her go to bed at 9:00 p.m., which she didn't like, wanting to be treated like Erica. It must have been hard being the middle child, not wanting to be a kid but not old enough for teenage privileges.

Kayla wanted to sleep when she wanted and claimed she would live outside if she wanted to. I didn't understand why she seemed to hate being here so much. What had I done? Maybe we should have stayed in Omaha. Maybe this move had been too difficult a transition for her. Kayla said she loved being back in Iowa, so why was she giving me so much trouble?

On multiple nights Kayla would spend her sleep time right outside my bedroom door. Usually when she was trying to pick a fight. Maybe this was an attention-getting ploy. She would take paper and rip it outside my door and chant about something she wanted.

"Late," Kayla would chant in a low, monotone voice that almost had a hiss to it. Riiiiiiiip would go the paper as she slowly pulled it apart.

"Late," she would hiss again, followed by a riiiiiiiiip.

"Late."

The actions were rhythmical and went on for hours. I didn't understand how Kayla could even have brought herself to do this. I would have gotten bored. It was actually a little scary. I would usually jump on text with Brenda, Kayla's counselor at the time.

"Kayla is chanting again," I would text Brenda.

"IGNORE IGNORE!" she would text back.

"I know, but it's so hard."

"She wants you to engage and start a fight. Keep giving her choices and consequences. She can go to bed when she wants to, but she needs to stay in her room."

"True, but how do I get her to stay in her room?!"

"Just continue to ignore her. She wants a reaction."

The next morning Kayla would seem back to normal.

"Good morning," I would say to her as she came downstairs.

"Ugh," was the typical reply. I would leave for work.

When I got home from work she would be her normal talkative self. On this particular day she did the dishes, and we were able to communicate with each other. Was this her way of apologizing? I chose not to bring up the previous night's occurrence. Hers was a roller coaster of behaviors.

August 6, 2015

We saw the kids' aunt over the weekend due to their missing their cousins. I believed that the aunt was still trustworthy. She didn't have a close connection with Abigail and avoided Stacy at all costs. The kids' aunt often commented that Abigail had never been much of a mom and that she herself had pretty much taken care of her siblings before leaving the home at a young age. She reminds me a lot of Erica.

Abigail was becoming consistently bothersome, wanting to know where we lived and what she had done wrong in that I hadn't allowed her to see the kids since February. I learned that Abigail hadn't stopped driving due to her medications, as she had previously claimed. Abigail had lost her license due to driving intoxicated.

I also learned that Abigail and Stacy were seeing each other on a regular basis and going drinking together. I did not believe that Abigail wanted to see the kids based on her missing them but due to Stacy's bugging her. I also learned that when the kids were in a foster home Abigail had posed as a family worker and thereby gotten into the school.

I had taken the proper precautions and had notified our school and the police station. The police station had me fill out a statement. They were in the process of securing for their files pictures of Abigail, Stacy, Chad, and Trinity and would give copies to the school for their files. The police also took school pictures of the children so they could keep an eye out for them on the streets.

I wanted to believe that Abigail wouldn't be stupid, but I wasn't taking any chances. She still didn't know where we lived. However, I worried now that we had seen the aunt that the situation might change: the kids telling the cousins, the cousins slipping up, etc.

CHAPTER 38

Kayla's Contract

August 9, 2015

Kayla was agitated and looking to fight with everyone. She lost her pool privileges due to her aggression and mean behavior. She kept telling me she didn't need parents and that she wasn't going to follow rules, that she could eat whatever she wanted, sleep whenever she wanted, and live outside if she wanted to.

"I'M GOING TO RUN AWAY!" was the new threat she liked to toss my way.

She cleaned out her room of belongings and put them in a get-rid-of pile that we maintain for our local donation center. Kayla wanted to live and eat in her bedroom. This wasn't the first time this had happened or the first time she had said she didn't want to live with me. She insisted that she wanted to go back into foster care.

Kayla wrote up a contract that I was supposed to fill out and left it outside my bedroom door.

"QUESTIONS

How much for rent? $_____

Can I eat and drink in room? Circle yes or no

You don't pick my bedtime, I do!

NO COUNSELORS THEY SUCK AND DON'T HELP

If I eat/drink in my room then I need a little fridge.

If you don't get this, then I WILL!"

I responded back with a return letter to her:

"Kayla,

I love you very much. I understand that you want to make your own rules and be independent. However, you are only 11. Too young to get a job, and too young to pay rent. You are old enough to follow rules and have consequences for inappropriate behavior. You can get rid of what you want and keep what you want in your room.

You have to make a choice:

Choice 1: You will be respectful to me and others, have a bedtime, follow household rules, and show responsibility. You can hang with friends and have extracurricular activities.

Choice 2: You can keep acting disrespectful and I can keep documenting your behavior. If you continue to behave this way then the law says you have to live with the other parent, Scott. I don't want that for you, but if you hate it here so much then that is our next step.

You are much loved, Kayla, and I wish you would accept it. I love you and wish you will choose choice 1. Love Mom"

I chose to make a copy of this letter for documentation. I really hoped that seeing this in writing would help her visualize the consequences and the benefits of each of her two options.

I left my bedroom and deposited my letter outside her bedroom door and tiptoed back to my room. Within a minute or two I heard her opening her door. Another minute passed by. I then could hear ripping paper coming from the hallway. So much for that.

I did confide in Collin about the weird behaviors Kayla had been exhibiting,

"Kayla has always been a handful," Collin said. "I'll never forget trying to get her ready for school. Sometimes it would take a few of us to get her ready. She would be throwing a huge temper tantrum, and we would have to wrestle her to the ground just to get her shoes on. Then she would pop up like nothing had happened, give us hugs goodbye, and head out the door."

CHAPTER 39

New School Year, New Relationships

August 24, 2015

The school year had started! Ethan started football and was excited. Erica refused to do cross country, I think due to being in a new school. Once she warmed up, I assured myself, she would take off. Kayla was going to start 4-H soon, and I was trying to get her into a sewing class offered by the local quilt shop. We would keep plugging along, one day at a time, trying to focus on the good.

September 4, 2015

The kids and I continued to get together with Collin. Kayla did better when Collin was around. She didn't get violent and was respectful. Maybe she was worried about my own and Collin's relationship that we, from her perspective, either could or could not pursue. I am not even sure, looking back, what we were or were not doing at the time.

We kept our feelings for each other at bay in front of the kids, unsure how they would react. We did secretly hold hands and had had our first kiss. I felt we had a deep connection.

Journal Entry

Collin is patient, kind, and comforting. He has been helpful with the kids, supportive, and hasn't been judgmental. He already impresses the kids and is a good role model for Ethan. Are we moving too quickly? Is this a game? I don't want to get my hopes up that maybe we have a relationship starting and then dash it in front of the kids.

I decided that Collin and I really needed to talk about it. I was anxious at the thought that maybe this relationship idea was just in my head.

After work I texted Collin: "We need to talk."

I shook as I texted. I didn't want to lose what we had but couldn't keep on doing this if it was all just a game. I really liked him, and such a complication would make things weird with the kids.

"Okay, I'll call you later," Collin replied.

"No, I want to talk face-to-face. It's important. Can we meet tomorrow?" I didn't want to have this conversation over the phone. I wanted to get this over with, but I knew he was back in Osceola by now.

"No, I'll come over tonight."

"Aren't you back in Osceola?"

"Yes, but I'll come back."

We met at the local park so we could talk in private. I told the kids I was going to run a couple of errands and would be right back. They looked at me quite suspiciously as I ran out the door, trembling inside.

When I got to the park we sat on the bench. "Thanks for meeting me tonight," I said.

"Yeah, well, you have me worried," Collin replied. "Being we need to talk face-to-face."

"I didn't want to have this conversation over the phone," I anxiously said. "What are we doing? I don't want to start something if you aren't in this for the long haul. My life is a circus with the kids. We can't play games. If you don't see a serious relationship out of this, then I don't want to play the game and hurt the kids in the long run."

"Oh, good! I thought you were calling it off!"

Collin smiled at me: "I want to join your circus. When you and Scott adopted the kids a few years ago, I saw them for the last time before they went to Omaha. They left and I cried. I really thought that was going to be the last time I saw the kids. I want to join your circus. I love those kids."

I smiled back at him. This made my heart so happy! I felt joyous inside! This was the first time in a long time that I had felt happy and excited about life. I couldn't believe the route God had put me on! The courage to leave Scott, the destination of Leon, and the weird connection Collin and I had through the kids! The best part was that the kids and Collin already knew and loved each other. God works in mysterious ways!

September 6, 2015

A few days went by, and Collin came to visit. We decided to tell the kids that we are dating.

The kids were excited but acted as though they were not surprised about this.

"Hey, you guys remember when you used to give me tips on how to pick up girls?" Collin asked them.

"Yes! We said, 'You'll have to get her flowers and probably beer,'" Kayla giggled.

"Blue Moon!" exclaimed Ethan.

Over the coming days, when we told our families and some friends that we started dating, they all exclaimed, "IT'S ABOUT TIME!"

I guess it had been no secret that we liked each other.

November 15, 2015

Carol released Ethan to try visits with Scott again. She believed he was doing much better on his current medication. Kayla continued to have outbursts, and some nights she still conducted her séance outside my door. Erica seemed to be doing well, unless I was still missing something.

Scott was unsupervised with the kids on Friday for about seven hours due to his intended supervisor having had an emergency come up. The kids were uncomfortable but too scared to say anything—except for Ethan, that is.

Ethan told me when they were back home, "I said to Scott, 'Shouldn't you be supervised?' Scott said, 'What do you think?' I told him, 'Yes, you should be supervised.' Scott just said 'Huh.' What does he think, that I'm not going to tattle?"

I had to laugh at Ethan.

Scott should have called someone else for backup, as there were plenty of people in the area we had decided together would be qualified supervisors. I was in the area too, and he knew it; he could even have called on me. My guess is that this wasn't the only time the kids had been alone with him.

The kids were telling me all the time that his family members would regularly leave them alone for a while. I understand that the family couldn't supervise Scott all the time, but the kids were uncomfortable, as Scott could blow up about anything unexpectedly, as he had done in the past.

They were too scared to tell Scott how they felt for fear he would get mad. I didn't know what to do, fearing that law enforcement wouldn't do anything until he actually lost his cool and hit someone again. My chest filled with anxiety.

CHAPTER 40

Mediation and Reunification

November 23, 2015

The divorce was final! Scott had given up the custody battle, and, according to my lawyer, the child support "became more favorable" for me. Scott and I had both signed the papers, and we were waiting for the judge to sign them. I could not believe how long the process had taken! Scott continued to lie and deceive, and the kids and I continued to distrust him.

The kids were scheduled for their first meeting with the reunification counselor on Wednesday and were not happy about it. I was trying to convince them of how important it was to communicate with the reunification counselor, even though they didn't want to rebuild their relationship with Scott. I kept telling them that she would be their advocate to the court if the relationship became unamendable.

There was one thing that Scott and I had always agreed upon: Abigail and Stacy were not trustworthy! Abigail was so upset that we weren't allowing her to see the kids any longer that she wanted to go to a mediator. Scott and I agreed, so we met Abigail at a lawyer's office.

"I feel like I'm on trial here," Abigail said as we laid out some ground rules with the mediator.

If she were to see the kids on a regular basis again, there would have to be no more talk about how they should see Stacy. she was to be supervised on her visits, and there would be no more drinking alcohol in front of the kids.

Abigail would be allowed to see the kids monthly, alternating a weekend with me one month followed by a weekend with Scott the next. This meant that I would have to deal with the fallout from the kids only six times a year.

I felt better now that there were rules in writing that she would have to follow if she wanted to continue seeing the kids on a regular basis. We were making progress; however, I wondered how long it would be before Abigail would start the next shenanigan.

December 4, 2015

Wednesday had come, and we met with the reunification counselor. We were all nervous, as we didn't know what to expect when we got there. We sat in the lobby, where there were toys galore. Kayla and Ethan took off to play, while Erica and I sat and waited.

The counselor, Linda, came out of her office. She introduced herself, and I introduced the kids. I gave her the divorce decree, pointing out the paragraph that stated what needed to be done.

"It reads as though you don't have to come, Heather," she responded. "This is reunification for Scott and the kids to rebuild their relationship."

"Okay."

"I'll take the kids in one at a time to get to know them. Then in a few weeks we will meet together with Scott. He has already been here for his one-on-one."

The kids went and saw her one by one. Each came out looking like a beaten dog. I hated putting them through more counseling. They should be off playing.

December 15, 2015

Kayla was severely angry and depressed. We visited with our primary care doctor. He was really disturbed by what he was hearing about our situation.

"May I call your reunification counselor and see what her thoughts are?" he asked.

I looked at Kayla. She just shrugged her shoulders as though she didn't care.

"Sure," I replied.

"Based on what she says, I would like to write a letter to whomever it may concern how detrimental it is for Kayla to see Scott," the doctor continued.

"Okay, I would appreciate that."

We left. In the afternoon the nurse gave me a call.

"Your primary doctor called Linda, your reunification counselor, today. Linda told him that she would like to meet with Scott and the kids a few times before she writes her letter of why the visits should be discontinued. He said he is happy to write a letter if or whenever you may need it."

"Okay, thank you." I hung up the phone feeling a little more empowered. If I could get professionals to help, maybe we could get the court to see that this was not going well. Then we would hopefully be able to move on.

CHAPTER 41

Who Is Lying?

December 20, 2015

Scott had put it together that Collin and I were dating. Over the weekend he had cornered Erica. Hours later, after I had picked her up, she was still fuming about the confrontation.

"Scott asked me all kinds of questions. He wanted to know if you are sleeping in the same room together and if Collin stays over often."

"Oh. Did you tell him that it's none of his business?"

"Scott said he thought it was too early for you to be dating. He was wondering if it made me uncomfortable that you're dating."

"Does it?"

"NO! And I did tell him it was none of his business. I like Collin and am happy you two are together. I got so mad I walked away from him."

Erica got really upset just talking about it. She fumed around the kitchen like a little tornado.

"I'm done putting myself down for him," Erica finished before storming away to her room. I think she was trying to say she was tired of not sticking up for herself or giving Scott boundaries.

Later I went up to her room and told her to write down the detail and give it to the reunification counselor. I sent a text to Brenda, the girls' regular counselor, to let her know what was going on.

December 22, 2015

Kayla was being defiant again. She was refusing to do chores, was rude to all of us, and was trashing things. We were walking on pins and needles. Brenda suggested that I call the police to start getting her behavior documented. I tried a new tactic instead.

"Kayla, if you keep this behavior up, your next option will be living with Scott," I informed her, hoping this wouldn't completely backfire.

She snarled, "Good, I want to leave."

"If that makes you happy, then you could go with him today," I responded, calling her bluff.

"I want to go."

I wrote a text to Scott stating that she wanted to live with him and would pack her things.

Before sending it, I showed her the text, only to receive the response, "I don't care—send it."

So I did.

Within a few minutes Scott called; he was being "all nice" and wanted to take Kayla for the week of

Christmas break. During the whole conversation I was thinking, *This is a bluff—she isn't really going.*

Scott proceeded to inform me, "Erica came to me over the weekend and expressed that she was uncomfortable that Collin and you were dating and how she thought it was too soon."

OH, WHAT THE HELL?!

"I know that you're lying. Erica told me everything, and I told her counselor. The counselor said this is none of your business. If Erica really had a problem with it, she would have said something to someone months ago when we started dating! Just stay out of it!"

"You have to watch Erica. She is playing you," Scott started.

I cut him off before he could say more: "Do you want to speak to Kayla or not?"

He continued to talk about Erica, and again I cut him off: "I need a yes or no answer." I was ready to hang up on him.

"Yes," Scott responded; he proceeded to say something else, but I took the phone away from my ear and walked upstairs to Kayla. She was packing, and I handed her the phone.

I didn't stay to listen in on the conversation. I went across the hall and knocked on Erica's door.

"Come in," she invited.

I stood in the doorway as she was cleaning her room and putting clothes away.

"Scott just told me that it was you who came to him this weekend about Collin's and my relationship," I told her. Immediately she was furious.

"How dare he put this back on me?!" Erica yelled.

"I don't know what to tell you," was all I could get out as Kayla came back out of her room and handed me the phone. I brought it up to my ear. Shoot, he was still there.

"I'll take Kayla. I promise not to yell. I'm also sorry for my earlier comments."

WTF Dr. Jackal, Mr. Hyde!!! We hung up.

I gave Kayla and myself a few minutes before I went into her room. Brand new child!!! She was sitting on the edge of her bed playing with her camera. I sat down with her, putting my arm around her, and we had a coming-to Jesus talk. How I love her and don't want her to go, but that if this is what she wants I would do what she needed to make her happy.

We shared some tears, and she finally said, "Since Scott has left I can't love anyone for fear that they are going to leave me. So instead of loving, I push everyone away, including my siblings."

"That makes sense, Kayla, given what you have been through all your life. You were abandoned at a young age and afraid you will be abandoned again. We will keep working with Brenda to see if she can help you learn to trust others again."

CHAPTER 42

Weird Sleeping Arrangements

December 24, 2015

The last couple of days Kayla had been golden—like the old Kayla. She did the dishes!!!!! I really hoped her new attitude would continue. She even got up out of bed on her own and was eager to start the day. We decided together that Kayla didn't need to go with Scott during Christmas vacation any longer. Maybe giving her the fear that I would follow through on sending her would be enough to make her snap out of it.

December 30, 2015

Over Christmas break Collin and I had a few days off. The kids and I ended up staying the night at Collin's house after we'd had a Christmas gathering with his parents. The kids were excited to have a slumber party there.

Being that Collin was a neighbor of Kyle and Megan, the kids wanted to invite Ryker and Kelly. Kelly was babysitting for the night, but Ryker came up. After an evening of games and movies, Ryker asked if he could spend the night, too. The weather was getting a little yucky, and he would sleep with Ethan in one room while the girls slept in a spare room. Collin and I were fine with that. Besides, this was what they did on Scott's weekends.

Once we got the kids settled down, we went to bed also. I could hear giggling and hushed whispers coming from the spare rooms. I went out and found all four kids trying to sneak around and stay up later.

"Time for bed, you guys—it's late," I called. I put Ethan to bed and tucked him in. He looked like a zombie and was already half asleep. Ryker joined him on the floor.

"Thanks for letting me stay, Heather," Ryker said.

"Sure, I hate to have you walk home this late, even though it's not that far."

I went back to bed.

I had just started to doze when I heard footsteps in the hall. Maybe someone was going to the bathroom. I was just starting to doze again when I heard voices. *Oh, come on!*

I went to the hallway quietly, figuring I would see all the kids again. No one. I went into the room the boys were sleeping in. Only Ethan was in there sleeping. I got a strange, sick feeling in my stomach.

I went into the girls' room and could hear shuffling in the bed while I flicked on the light. There lay Erica,

Ryker, and Kayla, all in the same bed! Ryker was in the middle, and the covers were up to their chins. My immediate gut reaction was that I didn't like a boy in the same bed with the girls!

"What's going on in here?" I asked harshly.

"We're just talking," Kayla snapped rudely.

"I told you it was bedtime," I replied.

Ryker and Erica were silent.

"We're just talking," Kayla repeated in the same tone.

Ryker was like an older brother to them, but I still had a weird feeling.

"Ryker, it's time for you to go home."

"Okay," he said with no objection, getting out of bed. They were clothed. My pulse came back down.

"Text me when you get there so that I know you're safe." After all, I had known him since he was six years old. I still saw him as my nephew.

The next morning Collin gave the girls a consequence of cleaning his house for not having followed the rules the night before.

"THAT'S NOT FAIR!" Kayla shouted. "How come we have to clean YOUR house? We didn't make your mess!"

Neither Collin nor I engaged. The girls proceeded to clean.

Ryker stopped by before the kids and I left.

"I'm sorry for not doing what I was supposed to last night," Ryker told us.

"That's okay," I replied. They were all good kids.

CHAPTER 43

The Kids' Honesty with Scott

January 12, 2016

We went to our reunification session for Scott and the kids. Scott was upset that I wasn't joining in. "The dissolution says WE have to go to reunification," he protested.

"Yes, you and the kids go to reunification."

"NO. It says WE need to work on reunification, which would include YOU."

"Heather doesn't need to reunify with the kids," the reunification counselor put in.

Scott was confused, as well as certain that he and I were expected to reunify too. WHAT?! Did he not understand what a divorce is?

It sounded as though the kids laid it all on the table at the reunification meeting. When they were done they came out into the lobby. For some reason the conversation continued with Scott, Linda, and the kids.

The kids told Scott in no uncertain terms that they don't want to see him. They felt that they didn't need to form a relationship with Scott because they had Collin . . . and had never had a real relationship with Scott.

"You change when you get around other people and put on a show," Kayla said to Scott.

"I don't like it when Russell supervises, and I want Megan to do it," Erica commented. "I do not want to go back to Omaha to visit at your house for a long time because I don't trust that Russell will supervise."

All the adults listened to the kids' requests in silence. It was best to allow them to vent.

In the waiting room they looked beaten, but by the time we got out of Scott's presence they perked back up.

Ethan told me in the car, "Scott just wanted to know if Collin and you were sleeping in the same bed."

That was none of Scott's business. Why would he bring that up in reunification?

The kids told me they were to draw pictures of who was in their family.

"I drew the three of us going into Russell's house with bubble sayings of not wanting to go and being scared to go," Erica divulged.

"I drew the angry character from 'Inside Out' and labeled him Scott, and we were all scared," Ethan reported. "Scott drew him and you together, holding a bow like a trophy and us next to you."

"Scott drew *me*?" I asked.

"Yup," confirmed Ethan.

Kayla said, "I drew you, Ethan, Erica, me, and a guy with a question mark. The counselor asked why Scott had a question mark above his head. I said, 'That's not Scott, its Collin!'" at which Kayla proceeded to laugh really hard. She seemed to be enjoying herself.

"I put the question mark above Collin's head because I was too scared that Scott was going to blow up!" Kayla continued with a chuckle.

"Linda pointed out that our pictures were similar in that us three are always together," Erica remembered.

The ride back home was good. They seemed relieved that they had gotten a lot of things off of their chests. I hoped that their courage would continue, but I was sure there would still be anxiety as feelings erupted that they didn't know what to do with.

Ethan whispered to me that evening privately, "Collin is so much better than Scott. Collin actually does things with me."

"Share that in in reunification so that everyone is aware," I told him.

"We are not allowed to talk about Collin in reunification," Ethan replied.

Journal Entry

We will be going to reunification weekly now. I'm hoping that within the month if it isn't working Linda might conclude that and we can stop going. Then I will go back to the court with counselor letters in hand. I will get a mediator who is a mental health professional and involved with the law and try to end visits. I just wish Scott would sign off on his rights.

January 19, 2016

I composed a letter to Linda, our reunification counselor:

"Kayla is giving Scott and me a lot of trouble. Scott and I stood firm together on a consequence last weekend and gave her choices. She made a choice, and was trying to play us, but we stood together and gave the consequence.

Last night I had to call the police. I had them come over to talk to her. Her name calling and defiance are out of control, and I was informed by Kayla's counselor that if I ever needed help to call them. Even after the police left she still had an attitude and showed no remorse. Kayla has told Ethan and Erica that you (Linda) have said she doesn't have to go to reunification anymore. Kayla says those things to make the other two kids feel that she is more special than they are or superior to them.

I'm not sure what you said, but I do know that Kayla takes whatever is said and twists it to her advantage. She does that to a lot of people. I'm letting you know this because there will probably be attitude again tonight at your meeting. Ethan was quite shocked that I followed through with the police call, and he will definitely talk about it.

Overall, I believe the visit over the weekend with Scott went well. I don't know if Kayla's outbursts are situational or if there are more underlying problems. She keeps saying how much she hates living with me, so I have told her that her only other option would be to live with Scott, and, well, I really don't want that.

I am working with Brenda, Kayla's counselor, on this. If you have any input at all in terms of what you see, I would be happy to hear it. I'm at the end of my rope with Kayla and need all the help I can get!"

After our session that evening Linda pulled me over to the side and said, "I will keep an eye on Kayla and her exchanges with Scott. In the meantime, keep working with her regular counselor." I thanked her for her time.

CHAPTER 44

Kayla's Downhill Spiral

February 9, 2016

Kayla continued to demonstrate lots of anger and aggression. The previous week she had taken a pair of scissors and cut her arm. We started Kayla on seeing a psychologist, Dr. Volga.

"Cutting is a coping mechanism. It's just a very poor choice for coping. Don't make a big deal out of it," Dr. Volga counseled.

Brenda and the school counselor had suggested the same thing. Brenda also decided to increase the frequency of their sessions to once a week.

March 1, 2016

After my continuously having a rough time with Kayla and talking to Brenda, she composed a letter to Dr. Volga:

"I want to touch base with you on Kayla. She has been on an antidepressant for several weeks now and, while it seemed to help her some initially, her behaviors and feelings seem to be getting worse. I met with her today, and she reports that she is not sleeping well at night. She reports she takes Melatonin and still only gets 4–5 hours of sleep. Kayla states that she stays up late and can't get to sleep or stay asleep. She continues to rage at home, yelling and calling names, destroying things in her room, and generally being extremely disruptive.

Per Heather, her perception of reality seems to be askew, as she recalls situations very differently from how they actually occurred. Kayla exhibits a lot of hopelessness and self-deprecating thoughts. She is very manipulative with friends and other adults and has a strong need to control others.

Kayla gets along fairly well in school but explodes when she is at home. I have given Heather guidance on different ways to handle her behaviors, but nothing seems to be working. I have spoken to the reunification counselor, and she states that minimal progress has been made there.

Kayla remains very angry. Today during our session she cried for the first time, which I thought was encouraging because she was expressing an emotion other than anger. She cut on her arms a month ago but hasn't had any self-harm incidents since.

Kayla's biological mother and biological grandmother have both been diagnosed with Borderline Personality Disorder. While I'm not willing to rule this out, I'm reluctant to diagnose this at this time until we have been able to rule other things out.

When she was evaluated by Dr. Johnston, he indicated there was some question about Bipolar Disorder, though this wasn't diagnosed either. I'm wondering if it might be beneficial to try a mood stabilizer with Kayla. I don't like the idea of pumping kids full of meds they don't need, but she seems to be getting worse. I think it would be worth pursuing this further. and if she doesn't respond to mood stabilizers we may need to look further into a personality disorder. I realize situational stressors and her age are also at play here, but she seems to be responding in a more intense way than a typical child her age would."

March 2, 2016

Kayla was communicating with her school counselor but telling her different things from what she was telling Brenda. Kayla had seen Brenda earlier that day and then went to the school counselor immediately afterward. Within an hour of Brenda's sending me an email that they'd had a session together, the school counselor was calling me.

"Kayla came to me today. I think the two of you are miscommunicating. Maybe you should get together with her regular counselor and talk," the counselor suggested, obviously trying to be helpful.

"Oh," I said. "Did Kayla tell you she had just seen Brenda?"

"NO, Kayla didn't say that," she replied. "Well, that's strange."

"I will definitely bring it up to Brenda and see if that is a path we should take," I reassured her, but I was sure Kayla was manipulating the school counselor.

"Brenda and I are discussing a mood stabilizer for Kayla," I continued. "She could possibly have bipolar or BPD, but we have a long road ahead of us yet."

"OH, I had no idea." Of course she wouldn't. Kayla would have left out some important stuff.

"It takes a village to raise a child, and I think I'm going to need a pretty big village with my kids!" I said jokingly. "Thank you for your call."

Kayla continued to act out that evening as we went to see Linda. A full day of counseling had to have been hard on her.

On the way home Kayla got after Ethan for something and was trying to control him, which led to an argument between the two. To break up the argument I simply said, "Kayla, just like you don't want to be controlled, neither does Ethan."

That was the wrong thing to say.

"I HATE LIVING WITH YOU! I DON'T WANT TO BE CONTROLLED BY YOU ANYMORE!" Kayla screamed.

She was sitting in the middle seat, so I could see her perfectly in my rearview mirror. She had a wild look in her eyes, as though she were completely out of control. Erica and Ethan just stared at her.

"YOU WOULD RATHER HAVE ME DEAD! I should just kill myself!" she continued.

"Kayla, that's not true . . . , " I tried to reason with her.

"I'm doing this so I can go to the mental hospital and not live with you anymore!"

I tried hard not to engage any longer. I realized there could be no reasoning with her. She did calm down and sat by the window then with her head buried in her arms. We were home by that point, and I simply ignored her as she stormed around the house. I felt awful for doing so because I knew she needed love, but the more I tried to love her the angrier she got.

I informed Brenda of my discussion with the school counselor and let her know that I would be happy to sign a release for the two of them to communicate together. I knew that the girls regularly went to see the school counselor during the week because she had called me before with concerns. I was going to keep my head up and keep fighting for Kayla even though she didn't want me to!!!

Brenda replied in an email:

"Kayla may have to end up in the hospital if this continues. She told me today she wants to go back into foster care. I pointed out to her that her issues would go with her (didn't word it exactly that way, but that was the message). She thinks she isn't loveable, I believe (which isn't your fault), and tries to

destroy any loving relationship she has or could have. I hope her psychiatrist will change her meds, and hopefully we'll see some improvement. I'm glad she is talking to the school counselor, and I will touch base with her if that's okay with you. But you're right—she is manipulating all the adults in her life right now. I think you handled the situation with her and Ethan as well as you could."

The rest of that night Kayla was really dark. She regularly experienced rough nights after seeing counselors. I didn't understand whether the thought process shook up old memories, possibly based on PTSD, or whether the counselors caught on to her manipulation and tried to get her to see things differently.

Kayla was trying really hard to pick a fight with Ethan. Her goal was clearly to get Ethan into trouble. They were fighting upstairs in the bathroom. Kayla was screaming, "Ethan, you're being mean. GET OUT!!!!"

Ethan was arguing back at her, "NO, I'M NOT! I WAS HERE FIRST!!"

I knew that Ethan had been there first, because he had just gotten finished with a shower. Kayla was trying everything in her power to get him into trouble. She even went so far as to put dirty dishes in his room and blame him for eating food there, when she herself was the one eating the food.

I quietly slipped upstairs to see Ethan in the bathroom doing his hair or something in the mirror. I watched as Kayla came in behind him and tried to push him out of the way.

Kayla climbed onto the edge of the bathtub and started hanging over him to get between him and the mirror. "GET OUT OF THE WAY! STOP BEING MEAN!"

Ethan yelled "KNOCK IT OFF!" and pushed Kayla.

She lost her balance backward and fell straight back into the tub wall, trying to grab on to something on her way down. She made contact with the shower curtain. As she slid down the wall, she had a surprised look on her face, and she took the curtain and the rod down with her. Ethan rarely stood up to his sisters. They regularly bullied him around.

Collin saw it too, and we couldn't help but laugh. Kayla was not injured. She did sit in the bathtub pouting, though.

Collin asked her in a kind but joking way, "Did you break your butt? It has a crack in it?!"

Kayla was furious that Ethan wasn't getting into trouble for pushing her. I tried to help her decompress and volunteered to go with her to her room to cool off. She got out of the bathtub and went to her room. I tried to join her but she shut the door in my face. Sigh.

CHAPTER 45

Temporary Home

March 3, 2016

While Kayla was in school I decided to go through her room. I didn't make a habit of going through the kids'; private things, but I had a hunch that things were not going well for Kayla, was concerned, and was looking for verification.

I went through books and journals and finally came across a notebook she had been using for journaling. In there I found a list of all the people she thought were untrustworthy. It included basically everyone she knew. Kayla wrote that everyone would be better off without her and expressed that she wanted to die. *Oh, my poor girl!*

I contacted Brenda right away. She made a couple of phone calls, while I packed a bag for Kayla and myself. I called Collin to let him know what was happening. He said he could be at the house for Erica and Ethan when they got home.

Before I knew it, Brenda told me to pick up Kayla from school. I didn't want to make a big scene at school, so I told the office I was taking her in for an appointment.

After I picked up Kayla, I told her in the car, "I found your journal. I'm sorry that you are hurting so much. We are going to a Des Moines hospital to the ER department." Brenda told me to take her to Des Moines because this hospital included a mental health wing.

"WHAT?!" Kayla exclaimed.

"They will probably keep us there for a few days. They will be able to help you feel better," I continued. Kayla was silent.

It was an extremely quiet ride. I chattered idly, trying to get Kayla to engage. She chose to be silent. I imagined she was really mad.

When we got there I got her registered into the ER. They had known we were coming and had a bed ready for her! Shocker! Working in a hospital myself, I knew that they usually didn't have beds readily available for mental health.

Following the nurse to the psychiatric wing, we walked through the adult wing. Half of the patients looked like zombies staring at the floor, watching TV, or sleeping in various places. The other half stared at us like wild animals waiting to pounce on us, their fresh meat. It looked like a prison ward. Everyone was wearing matching scrubs, and we had to be buzzed through locked doors. I was a little freaked out. Where had I taken her?! I looked over at Kayla. She didn't seem surprised at all.

We got to the children's wing, which had the same look as the adult wing. The kids must have been in their individual rooms, as we didn't see anyone. They showed us to her room, and I settled in and started picking out my spot and familiarizing myself with the layout. Kayla settled into her gown while I started paperwork.

A nurse came in and started taking Kayla's vitals. I finished the paperwork and handed it in. I was curious what the rest of the wing looked like.

"Okay, being as you're done with paperwork, you can go home now, Mom," the nurse told me.

LEAVE?! WHAT? I'M SUPPOSED TO LEAVE HER HERE??

"I don't understand. I can't stay with her for a while?" I asked, bewildered.

"We will keep her here for a few days to make sure she is stable. She will have group counseling and individual counseling. Kayla will also see a psychiatrist, and they will get her on medication. She is in good hands here," the nurse explained.

How was I supposed to leave my girl there, by herself? Not knowing anyone . . .

"I'll be fine, Mom," Kayla assured me.

"Are you sure, Honey? I'm so sorry you are going through this."

"Yes, it's fine," Kayla replied coldly.

I reluctantly left. I felt hopeful that Kayla would get the help she needed, but also extremely sad. It was a long car ride home alone.

We were unable to visit Kayla the next day due to hospital rules. They wanted a day with her alone. We had a quiet night. I worried about her, yet it was a peaceful night at our house with no one fighting.

Journal Entry

I believe it wasn't a surprise to Kayla that she went into the hospital. I also believe she really wanted to be there. I found out from one of her friend's mothers that Kayla had told her friends that she was going to the hospital because she is mental.

I don't believe Kayla will keep her visit a secret, either. Actually, she may like the attention she will get for being in the "mental hospital." I have told some people in the community because it takes a village to raise a child, and I need the village to be bigger.

No one should ever have to fight mental illness alone, including the people on the front lines. Our family members are on a need-to-know basis at the moment. I don't need the kids' family coming out of the woodwork and passing their judgment on whether or not I did the right thing.

I believed this was going to happen no matter what. This is the way Kayla is wired. Yet I felt so guilty and sad. Kayla had to learn how to live with her emotions and control them, not let them control her. I had this problem also with my own anxiety and depression. How could I be a role model if I didn't know how to do it, either? Was I really a good fit for these kids?

CHAPTER 46

Was This the Right Move?

March 4, 2015

I talked to Kayla on the phone briefly at noon, and she still sounded monotone and angry.

"The bed sucks. It is rock hard, and they only give you one blanket," she informed me crossly.

My hope was that this experience might serve as a kind of a wakeup call to how good she truly had it at home.

March 5, 2016

We went with Collin as a family to visit Kayla in the hospital. The wing was full of teenagers, all having difficulty coping with life. They were all in a rec room that was full of board games, a foosball table, books, TV, and couches. A couple of the guys played foosball, while others were sprawled out on couches, lying around watching TV. It was Saturday, so presumably that was why they weren't doing anything more constructive.

We found Kayla sitting wonky in a chair with her legs spread apart, eating a Popsicle. She had free rein for food, which included access to a freezer full of popsicles and ice cream bars. She was in her "high" mood, in which she talks in a different voice and seems excitable—almost manic.

Kayla was extremely flirty with the boys playing foosball and was clearly not herself. At least she wasn't mean and crabby, I rationalized. The young lady that was there supervising them was barely out of high school. She sat in her staff T-shirt reading a magazine while the teenagers reminisced on how they had hurt themselves in the past and what trouble they had gotten into with the law. Kayla proudly showed off the scar on her arm where she had cut herself.

I glanced at Erica and Ethan, who both looked shocked at what they were seeing and hearing.

"So they just play around all day?" I asked the young supervisor, trying to be nonchalant and not overly sarcastic.

"They will have therapy on Monday," she replied, barely looking up from her magazine.

"So the weekend is a fun free-for-all?" I asked with obvious sarcasm.

I heard Collin whisper "Heather" kind of loud, trying to stop me and my tone.

The comment actually made the young lady look up.

"This is a suicide watch. Just making sure no one hurts themselves."

What had I done!? We basically put Kayla with others who were troubled like herself so she could get more ideas of what she might decide to pull next. We left shortly thereafter, and my heart was extremely heavy.

March 6, 2016

"Are you ready to come home?" I asked Kayla over the phone.

"NOPE."

Why would she be when she gets all the free food she wants, watches TV all day, and gets ideas about her next move! Not to mention that she doesn't have any chores.

"How come I don't have a menu to choose from at home so I can circle what I want like here at the hospital?"

"I am not a restaurant."

I didn't understand why she hated me so much that she didn't want to live with me. I feared that the hospital would do nothing for her beyond increasing her antidepressants, drugging her up, and offering her the power of suggestion.

March 7, 2016

I talked to the therapist on the phone.

"The results from her testing showed severe depression. We have added Abilify to the antidepressant she is already on," the therapist explained.

"I really think Kayla has something else going on, not just depression. She plans things and is . . . "

"We are here to treat the symptoms and make her stable," the therapist interrupted.

"But I read somewhere that antidepressants can make bipolar worse," I replied.

"You will have to talk to her psychiatrist to change her medication."

I was scared for Kayla that she would turn into a guinea pig and that her moods would continue to intensify. I also feared that sending her to the hospital had not been the right answer.

I later got another phone call, this one from a different young lady who was supervising the wing. "I'm having some problems with Kayla today that I want you aware of," she said. "Kayla is the only girl on the floor at this time. She has been doing a lot of attention seeking about her cuts and is very flirtatious with the boys. We are going to keep her separate or in her room for the rest of the evening."

Oh, thank goodness. Someone was actually paying attention and noticing the same things I was. Kayla had always been attention seeking and would say random things, even things that were untrue, or do something random to attract attention.

"Is this something you can document?"

"Yes it's in her chart. When we have difficulties and have to isolate, we contact the guardian or parent."

"Okay, thank you for letting me know."

I composed an email to Brenda about my concerns. She promptly responded back: *"I remain very concerned about Kayla, especially with the things she is saying about not wanting to come home. It concerns me that she is going to try things to get put back in the hospital. I'm looking into longer term options for her, such as a PMIC (Psychiatric Medical Institute for Children). There aren't a lot around, but there are some. I emailed your reunification counselor to see if she could give me more info on the one in Des Moines. I think you need to keep a close eye on her and continue to make sure anything dangerous is kept away from her as best you can. I'll be in touch as soon as I know more."*

I responded to Brenda: *"I couldn't agree with you more, Brenda! It is almost like she enjoys causing trouble at home and the negative attention this is all getting her. She wanted to go to the hospital and is enjoying it there. I am concerned that she will run away or hurt herself. Plus, I'm not sure about the medication they are putting her on. Please look into those places and let me know what I need to do on my end. Thank you."*

From Brenda: *"Kayla hates her life (and she has un-doubtedly been through a ridiculous amount of trauma), and since you are in her life you get the anger and hatred spewed on you as well. If I played your role in her life, she'd hate me too. It's not about what you are doing or not doing. It's an accumulation of everything that has happened with and to her."*

March 8, 2016

Kayla was still at the hospital and would possibly be released the following day. I went around our house looking for anything that could be dangerous and locking it up.

"Anything dangerous."

That could be anything! I locked up knives and scissors and all medications. Kayla's favorite thing to do at the moment was cut her arms.

I had addressed my fears about the Abilify with Kayla's psychiatrist. He said we could always up the dosage to turn it into a mood stabilizer.

I feared that Kayla would just keep being defiant, but to a worse degree, or hurt herself more. Kayla's moods had changed every time I had talked to or seen her in the hospital. Once she seemed back to her normal self, but at other times she was monotone and sad, and the previous afternoon she had been defiant and wanted to challenge me again. Her moods were so unstable.

I had noticed this for a while and thought the problem might be hormonal, but she seemed to keep getting worse, with more frequent outbursts. I would like to have thought I could handle this on my own, but I was starting to truly believe the situation was out of my realm. Loving her was not enough.

The situation was taking a toll on Erica and Ethan, too.

"I'm happy she's gone to the hospital—no drama!" Erica exclaimed.

Ethan cried on the Friday night that she wasn't home: "I feel bad for Kayla."

"I do too, Honey. I do too." I tried comforting Ethan, but he always shied away from hugs.

"I don't want her coming home tomorrow," Erica declared.

I was lost as to what to do next. I just keep bugging the counselors and psychiatrist. I felt constantly anxious. How could I help these kids when I was just as anxious as they were?

I talked to Kayla on the phone in the evening.

"I'm ready to come home," she admitted. "I feel like this new pill is increasing my self-confidence already! I don't know how to explain it, but I'm happy!"

This made me happy! As I thought more about her comment after we hung up, though, I realized that she had said the exact same thing when we had started her on the antidepressant and again when we had increased the dosage. The pharmacist said it would take about a month to notice a difference, and she had been on it for only two days. This, I realized, was a placebo response at this time, and the other shoe would drop again.

March 9, 2016

Collin and I went to pick up Kayla. My parents came over to the house and hung out with Ethan and Erica after school. While in the car home Kayla was saying again how much she loved the food there and wanted to stay for the food, though she hated the sleeping accommodations.

When we got home my mom gave Kayla a hug.

"Glad to have you back, Kayla," she welcomed her. "How was it there?"

"The food was terrible. It was worse than school food," Kayla replied.

She continued on about the bed, as I stood there in disbelief.

I didn't understand how she could say one thing to me and the exact opposite to someone else. Was this an attention getter, an age thing, or lack of confidence causing her to say whatever she thought would please someone?

Kayla told me later, "I want a different therapist. Brenda and I are friends, and it's hard to open up to friends. I like to open up to complete strangers instead."

"Well, if we did that, Kayla, we would have to keep switching therapists because they would all get to know you well and become like a friend. Why don't you think about it some more," I replied.

I believed she was attaching to Brenda and was scared of this reality. Or Kayla may have come to the realization that she couldn't manipulate Brenda any longer, since Brenda had her pegged.

Erica and Ethan were both either mad at Kayla or scared of her. I wasn't sure which. Neither really wanted to talk to her, since she has been so mean and angry with all of us. I wasn't sure whether they would eventually warm up but feared that she would blow again.

CHAPTER 47

Failed

March 10, 2016

I received an email today from Linda, our reunification counselor:

"Dear Heather and Scott,

This letter is to update you on progress that I have seen in our family therapy session and my prognosis for your family moving forward. We have had two separate intakes, one with Scott individually and one intake session that included time for all three children separately. We have also had five family sessions that included Scott, Erica, Kayla, and Ethan. The sessions have spanned from 11/4/15–2/6/16. During this time our goal has been to rebuild and improve the connection between Scott and the three children and to heal the trauma of abuse that occurred at Scott's hands.

Throughout our family session all three children have voiced that they do not want to build or have any relationship with Scott. They all continue to call him Scott. Each child has handled the visits differently. During our first sessions all three children talked about fears they have about Scott's anger. Scott struggled with understanding what situations the kids were feeling fearful about. We decided on a safe word for them to use in case they felt like Scott was getting angry, to let him know they were feeling fear over his reactions. Although they have reported there were times they felt the need to use the safe word, they chose not to use it as they thought it would make him angrier.

Scott has continued to struggle to understand what the kids are talking about when they tell him they have seen him get angry during visits. When they have confronted him in sessions about his yelling or anger, he will at first deny that it happened and then will end with saying "Okay, fine, I understand." It does not appear that he understands their concerns and is agreeing to what he thinks he is supposed to be agreeing to. Scott struggles with insight into, and taking responsibility for, his emotions and his reaction unless confronted multiple times.

There has also been a consistent difference of opinion about whether the three kids have enjoyed their time during the visit. Scott has talked about feeling as though the children have fun on the visits, smile, and enjoy the activities with him. Kayla has voiced that she hates the visits and does not want to go on them at all. Ethan and Erica have voiced some of the same thoughts. They have talked about enjoying some of the different activities and at the same time not feeling as though they are spending time being connected with Scott. It is the activities they enjoy, not spending time with Scott.

I have had some concerns about a family member who may be inadvertently sabotaging the visits. The children's aunt (Megan), who is one of the visit supervisors, has been a wonderful support for the kids. They have felt like she is always willing to listen to them and stand up for them. Unfortunately, at times when talking with the children about their concerns, instead of working to help Scott and the kids communicate about the issue she will get frustrated with Scott and just agree with the kids.

During the family therapy session there has been an intense disconnect between all family members except for Ethan. Scott, Kayla, and Erica will stare at the floor or off into space until a direct question is asked of them. They are all polite, and Scott, Erica, and Kayla all willingly participate, though they do not actively participate. There is minimal conversation that occurs. Ethan actively participates in conversation and has improved in the area of having a voice with Scott. However, he also continues to say he does not want a relationship with him.

The prognosis I see for this family moving forward is poor. The biggest block is that these three children did not have a relationship built up prior to the abuse occurring. Therefore, there is no solid foundation for us to rebuild these relationships on. That, coupled with the lack of desire from the children and the continued struggle Scott has with insight into his emotions and behavior, brings me to the conclusion that continued family therapy will most likely not be helpful or effective.

I have not witnessed Scott having the skills needed to build relationships with these children. Erica, Kayla, and Ethan came to this family through foster care with a trauma history. During his relationship with them he added to that trauma through the verbal and physical abuse that occurred. Scott has been unable to connect with the kids or instill a feeling of safety and security while they are with him. I believe that Scott would like to have a relationship with the children. That desire is not enough, however, to build that relationship at this point.

If the family decides to continue with family therapy, I am more than happy to continue working with them. If they feel that my services are not working well for them, I am also willing to give them referrals to other therapists. It will be important for all the children and Scott to continue in individual therapy and leave open the possibility for building a relationship in the future if the desire is there.

Thank you for your time and work to help your family heal. I wish for all of you health and healing in the future. Thank you for sharing your family with me.

Signed, Linda Reunification Counselor"

Once I received the email I sent it to Brenda and Carol, the kids' other counselors. I wanted them to read it and compose their own letters about what they were seeing from the kids. This would be good insight to send to Scott to let him know that things were not working and that we needed to reevaluate what we were doing.

CHAPTER 48

Social Media

March 23, 2016

As any teenager would want, Erica was after me for a phone. She was almost fifteen, so I guessed it was time. I reluctantly got her a phone and told her she could use Instagram only if she let me see it whenever I wanted to and I knew her passwords.

Within a few days Stacy found her on Instagram. Erica told me that Stacy had contacted her and given Erica her and Chad's phone numbers. Stacy told her she missed her and wanted to explain what had really happened and that she had been forced to give the kids away.

Erica was confused after this conversation, thinking that she might want to talk to her biological parents and hoping they might have changed. We talked about it, and I gave her the DHS paperwork, hoping to change her mind.

"Do you want me to go through the paperwork with you?" I asked.

"Sure," she replied.

I believed she was old enough to know what had really happened. Erica read through only a little bit of it with me. I think it was too much for her to handle. I left a copy of the paperwork with her so she could go back to it when she felt she needed to.

I contacted my informant about the biological family, advising them about Stacy having contacted Erica.

"Stacy is using meth again, and the family is trying to get her to go back to treatment. Stacy's wife, Trinity, wants to leave her again because she is tired of Stacy using meth," my informant told me.

I also contacted the kids' aunt. She agreed to give Erica a call and give her some insight into what she should do. I guess the phone call went well. The aunt reported that Erica understood why she couldn't see Stacy but did not understand why she couldn't see her dad, Chad.

Abigail also texted me later in the evening: "I heard that Stacy contacted Erica?"

I confirmed this and explained to Abigail through text what had happened.

"Oh, Erica didn't need this. I'm so glad she talked to a counselor. Somehow I have to make sure this doesn't happen again. Will you get a restraining order?"

"I don't know yet."

"I really hope you do; now that she is using again, I can't trust her anymore."

I had been informed by others that Stacy was a major manipulator, a triangulator, and that you could never believe anything she said. Stacy used people and coerced men into buying vehicles and gifts for her, even though she was married to Trinity. I contemplated getting a restraining order against her for the kids and myself, reprimanding myself that I shouldn't have gotten Erica that stupid phone.

CHAPTER 49

Trying to Communicate

March 28, 2016

I was compiling different letters to take to a mediator to look over our divorce agreement. We would meet again in a couple of months, as mandated in our decree. I really wanted the kids not to see Scott any longer and was hoping to reach an agreement in mediation without having to go to court. Court cost a lot of money. I just wished Scott could see how detrimental this situation was to the kids and let us go on without him in their lives.

Brenda sent me a letter to use for mediation:

"I'm writing at this time to provide a summary of my work with Erica and Kayla up to this point. I have had the opportunity to review letters written by Linda and Carol. I have been seeing both girls weekly to bi-weekly since August 2015. Both girls have experienced a high degree of anxiety and depression over the past several months. Erica was on an antidepressant for a period of time but seemed to do worse on it. Kayla has been on

an antidepressant and is now on Abilify as well, following a psychiatric hospitalization a few weeks ago.

I am aware that they have been attending supervised visits with Scott every other weekend since the fall of 2015 and have been participating in reunification counseling with Linda. It is my impression that neither of these girls feels bonded to Scott. They consistently express distress and frustration about being forced to go for visits with him. Both girls state that they don't trust Scott and have no desire to have a relationship with him. Despite my attempts to encourage them to be open to the possibility that things could be better between them and Scott, they remain steadfast in their feelings about him.

Linda's report seems to indicate that very little progress has been made in reunification therapy, and this sentiment is validated by the girls consistently. Kayla in particular seems to struggle with the visits with Scott. She demonstrates increased anger and acting out during the weeks she has a visit coming up. Both girls have self-harmed and admitted feelings of hopelessness about the situation with Scott.

Based on the fact that there doesn't appear to have been a bond to begin with, the trauma they have endured, and their consistent feelings about the situation, visits with Scott seem to be detrimental to them both. I believe this situation needs to be revisited and that the appropriateness of continuing visits and/or reunification counseling should be seriously considered.

Regarding their relationship with Heather, while it is conflictual at times, both girls seem to be bonded to her. Their issues with her seem to be more in the normal range and/or displaced frustration with other situations in their life over which they have no control. It is also worth noting that they both seem to have bonded with Heather's paramour, Collin. They have expressed very positive feelings towards Collin, which I found to be encouraging, considering they both have difficulties trusting males. Kayla, when asked to identify her "family," includes Collin and his dog on her list.

One other recent issue that needs to be addressed is contact Erica received from her biological mother, Stacy. Erica was very distressed this past Monday after receiving a message on social media from Stacy telling her how much she missed her, that she (Stacy) was forced to give them (Erica and her siblings) up, etc. This evoked a lot of confusion with Erica, as she desperately wants to believe she can have a healthy relationship with her biological parents. Unfortunately, it is reported that Stacy is using meth again and her wife recently left her. She is in no position to be a positive contributor to the lives of these children at this time and should not have any contact with them. This only facilitates false hope and confusion for these kids, and they need to be protected from this."

I composed an email to Scott: "This arrangement is not good for the kids, and I also feel it isn't good for your family to be in the middle.

I propose that you be supervised indefinitely. With that supervision I feel that you should look into purchasing someone to help with the supervision, not just your family. I also propose that we lower the visits to every three weeks instead of every other weekend.

I will give you until Friday morning 10 a.m. for a response via email. If I don't hear from you I will go ahead and contact a mediator."

March 29, 2016

Scott replied through email: *"I can't give you a definite answer until I have a chance to talk to the kids. FACE TO FACE. I am open to some change, and that will depend on my conversation with the kids. So after I talk to them I can tell you what I am open to."*

I replied, *"I'm not going to let you intimidate them and put them in the middle. They tell you on visits that they don't want to see you, and this should be no surprise to you based on the other letters. You have until Friday."*

Scott's response: *"You have been putting them in the middle for a long time. Kayla is the only one who has expressed not wanting to go. The other two have not said anything like that to me. **So after I talk to them** I can tell you what I am open to."*

"Then I suggest you Skype them," I replied. I was not going to let him intimidate them.

"You have my reply. And I believe any mediator will say that I'm still trying to work it out and that you are being unreasonable," Scott shot back.

I could almost hear the agitation in his voice, even though we were still communicating through email. I thought carefully before I typed my response: *"If you want to talk to them face to face, let's do it with Linda. I will set up an appointment. I don't want you having this face to face with them without proper supervision. Or you have my reply of going to mediation. I emailed Linda, and she is more than happy to do it. What week night works for you? Tomorrow night or Monday night works for me."*

"*Linda is unacceptable*," was his cursory response.

He was being impossible! I stopped replying in order to cool off. I was very anxious and having a hard time coping. The tightness in my chest was becoming just too much. Even through email he was giving me overwhelming anxiety.

March 31, 2016

A few days later I tried emailing Scott again: "*I need to know if you are open to mediation or not by tomorrow, Friday, April 1st. You do not need to talk to kids to see if you want to mediate. I did talk to a mediator. We are court ordered to mediate before going to court. If we do not have an agreement or an appointment for mediation scheduled by next Friday, April 8th, I will contact my lawyer. If you so desire to see the kids face to face before making a proposal, then you can pick a person to supervise the conversation who isn't a family member or me. Any counselors or maybe teachers would be happy to do it. I also just found out that Ethan's concert is Monday, April 4th, at 7:00 p.m., so we can easily set something up around 5:00 or so."*

Scott replied, "*I may be open to visits every three weeks instead of every other but only until January 1st, 2017. Since I am already not moved forward with the timeline yet based on* what the kids are okay with, the supervised visits will remain as it is written in the divorce papers and can be reevaluated at that time. And I have the right to have the kids this year for Christmas. This all depends on my conversation with the kids. I don't have a problem with mediation in Omaha at your expense, since you are giving demands and not suggestions."

UGH! I had forgotten I had to make him feel as though arrangements had been his idea. I replied, "*The mediation would be an even split, as the decree declares. I have contacted a mediator in Omaha, unless there is another mental health professional who is also a mediator that you would want to use. If you look at your decree, they have to meet those credentials. If you don't like this mediator, please choose one by Friday, April 8th. Also, if you look at the decree we are to mediate in August, so Jan 1st, 2017, cannot apply. It doesn't say we can't mediate before August, especially being that reunification has failed. I'm also wondering if you have completed your anger management program yet, as it is court ordered that I am to have proof of this completion too. My demands are my boundaries and a timeline so that you cannot abuse it like you did with the divorce. Who did you decide on for a supervisor for your talk with the kids?*"

I didn't receive a response back.

April 6, 2016

The kids had tried calling Scott the previous night to make yet another attempt to convey that they did not want to see him. After an epic phone fail, I composed another email. I liked this method of communicating so much better than talking face-to-face or even over the phone. I could keep my emotions in check plus have documentation of what had been said.

"You haven't answered who is going to be the non-family member who is going to supervise your visit with the kids and when that is going to be. Please let me know so I feel comfortable sending the kids this weekend.

Kayla and Ethan have very high anxiety about the weekend, as you should be able to tell from the phone call last night. They had high anxiety and wanted to tell you stuff that is bothering them. They made lists and prepared what they wanted to say and then called you. Then when they heard your voice, they got scared and angry at each other and didn't accomplish anything. The rest of the night and this morning they are angry, defiant, and sad. That is how they are for the full three to four days before they see you until about one day after seeing you. Just like how they used to react right before and after seeing Abigail, only worse.

They are not going to tell you that they don't want to come anymore, but they tell everyone else. I wish you would re-read the letters from the counselors and take into full consideration what the kids are going through and how much stress they are under. They are not going to tell you because they are terrified of the consequences and your anger. Please consider lowering the amount of time you see them and being continuously supervised without having to drag the kids into this adult matter. Maybe even consider stepping back and letting us go on our own. You wouldn't have to pay child support any longer. Please think of the kids and what this is doing to them."

Scott responded a short time later:

"*I have changed my mind about having the 'talk' with the kids. I had Dr. Jones lined up to be the supervisor for when I talked to the kids. They say one thing and they act another, so having 'the talk' would be useless.*

Mom and Russell will be the supervisors for the weekend. When does Kayla need her black boots by? This weekend we will be going to see Dr. Jones for a chiropractic adjustment Saturday morning. Saturday afternoon we will be meeting up with my aunt and uncle for some bow shooting and a visit (Russell and/ or Mom will be the supervisor). Depending on weather, we may get together with friends so the kids can play."

I replied, "*Thank you. I'm not sure what black boots Kayla would be asking for. As far as I know she doesn't need any. I have never heard about them. She is probably using you because she knows you like to buy them things. What do you want to do moving forward?*"

Scott replied, "*Kayla said she needed black boots for 4H. I don't know if she does or not—she said she did. Please let me know. As far as moving forward, let me talk to my family and get back to you. I do understand the anxiety. I wish you could see what goes on when they are with me. Last time Kayla intentionally sought me out to play her clarinet, twice, and talked to me about her friend Luke? Or Lance? I'm not sure. And how she defined her relationship with him and what to do about a Valentine gift. I just listened, and she came up with a very adult conclusion.*

Ethan shows me everything and wants to tell me all about school, sports, what he sees in the woods, and the list goes on and on. He does have a very hard time with no, and not just with me. I know that is not his entire fault—it's how he's programed.

Erica seem to be up for almost everything, except for a few instances when other things have been on her mind (Stacy, women things). They all want me to make up math problems for them almost every time and talk about snowmobiling, camping, and swimming in the creek.

It keeps me very confused as to what it real and what is not. So, after I talk to my family I will have a proposal plan."

I didn't know what to believe. Scott said one thing, and the kids another. Who knew?

CHAPTER 50

Breaking Point

Journal Entry: April 8, 2016

Kayla is heading right back down her path of destruction. She is becoming defiant and mean again. She isn't destroying anything yet, but I believe that is coming. Kayla told me that she took a borderline personality disorder test online and showed me that she scored 100% on having it. She also says she is fighting with friends because they call her a liar and fat. "I'm just an asshole," she said tonight. I'm worried about her again.

April 19, 2016

"Kayla, it's still your turn to do the dishes," I reminded her, pointing to the chore chart. She had refused to do them two days earlier. Instead of having one of her siblings do the dishes the following day to make up for her lack of responsibility, I left the dishes for her to do the next day.

She wasn't allowed to see friends or watch TV until she got them done. Maybe I shouldn't have reminded her. Maybe it was my tone . . . I tried to watch it, but every time there was any authority directed at her, she flipped.

"You can't make me. I'll do it when I feel like it!"

I wished I could just let it be that simple. We were out of dishes, and the kitchen was starting to stink.

"Kayla, I need you to do the dishes tonight or I will ground you for the week." I was going to leave it at that, but she somehow got my goat.

"I hate you. You wish I was dead! You are a stupid bitch, and you can't fucking tell me what to do!"

I don't remember precisely what else she said. I was trying hard to take deep breaths, but something exploded inside me. I lost all control of my words, my temper, my everything.

"I HAVE HAD ENOUGH! ENOUGH! ENOUGH OF YOUR BULLSHIT, ENOUGH OF YOU! I CAN'T DO THIS ANYMORE! I CAN'T TAKE ANYMORE!"

I started screaming. Screaming without words. I was slamming things around and basically throwing my own temper tantrum. I didn't know what else to do! The stress was too much! I was the one out of control now.

I was in the kitchen, and I slammed the cupboard door made of glass panels. As it slammed, the glass shattered and fell onto the counter and floor. I just screamed at it. I knew I had to calm down, so I went into the front room and sat in the chair and cried.

The next thing I knew, the police were knocking at my door. Erica greeted them at the door, and I met them there, too. Shame and guilt filled me. I knew I had done wrong.

"Hello, ma'am," the police officer said. "This young lady here got scared of your behavior and called us."

"I am sorry, officer. I lost my cool and was yelling and slammed the cupboard door," I admitted, ashamed.

"Did anyone get injured?" he asked.

"No," I replied, "It never got physical with each other. I was blowing off steam, but inappropriately."

"Are you the one she was mad at?" the officer asked Erica.

"No, Kayla is upstairs," Erica replied.

"Can she come down, please?" I went upstairs to retrieve Kayla.

"Kayla, the police are here and want to talk to you."

"Nope, I'm not going," Kayla replied in her high-pitched singsong voice as she sat at her desk. She had a child-size scissors and was cutting large grooves into her desktop. I took a mental note to find those scissors later.

I didn't want to take the risk of her injuring herself by forcing her downstairs, so I went back downstairs and told the officer that he could come upstairs instead. Oh, how I wished Collin were there. Maybe this wouldn't have happened.

The officer went into Kayla's room. She was not happy to see him. They had a long discussion about authority figures and how we may not like rules but need to follow them. I listened as the officer explained everything to Kayla—all the same concepts I had been trying to instill in the kids. It was refreshing to hear from the police that they were on the parental side of listening to authority.

Kayla informed him, "I don't like mother figures and being told what to do."

"Well, you will have to get over that. Even adults get told what to do."

The officer and I went back downstairs. He explained to me, "If it ever gets physical, charges can be filed."

"OH, NO!" I assured him, "That isn't going to happen. I won't get physical. I won't allow myself to get there."

"I mean on both ends," the officer clarified. He looked as though he wanted to give me more information and was implying something, but he didn't elaborate, most likely because Erica was standing there.

I was ashamed that I had lost my cool and had reached my breaking point. I didn't know what to do any longer. I'd had enough. I had tried to keep my cool and to reason with her, but I just couldn't continue.

April 20, 2016

I called the number Brenda had given me for the closest PMIC (Psychiatric Medical Institute for Children) and left a voicemail. I knew that when Stacy was twelve she had been placed in foster care—I believe because Abigail couldn't handle her.

I truly believed that Kayla had BPD, like Stacy, and that she was following in Stacy's footsteps. Stacy blamed Abigail for everything that had happened to her and didn't relate well to mother figures, either. Kayla was blaming me for things that had happened to her or blaming others for every decision she herself made.

I didn't want to send Kayla into foster care because I believed this was where Abigail had gone wrong. She had sent Stacy away instead of getting her the help she truly needed.

I emailed Brenda: *"How can you help me, Brenda? Can we get her diagnosed? Can you call the PMIC again? I need help. I don't want the opportunity to lose my cool again. I have never been that mad, and I need tools so that it doesn't happen again. Any input is appreciated. Is there any respite care in the area, even? Or when Kayla is completely out of control, what should I do? The officer said there is nothing they can do unless it becomes physical—that then they can press charges. I can't send her to the hospital unless she is hurting herself . . . What else is there?"*

How come everywhere I turned there seemed to be a dead end? Was the system supposed to be this confusing? Is that why some kids just run the streets— because the parents don't know what to do? I felt that I was failing as a mom. This wasn't how it was supposed to be. Scott and I were supposed to have taken the kids out of a bad situation and given them better. Then I needed to take them out of another bad situation with Scott. Now what? Was I going to end up being a bad situation for them, too?

CHAPTER 51

One Year Mark and a New Chapter

Journal Entry: May 12, 2016

Things are going. We have our ups and downs. Scott claims that he's okay with seeing the kids once a month due to the failed reunification but still wants them to visit his family every other weekend. So that is the routine we are following now.

I never heard back from the PMIC. It's annoying that they don't follow up. That's okay, though, because I don't think we need that big of a road. I'm taking a Nurtured Hearts class that was offered at the hospital, and the approach is totally different from the way I grew up. It is all about positive reinforcement only. Ignoring the bad behavior and only rewarding the good. Even if it is telling the child in the midst of a temper tantrum, "I am happy that you are breathing," your interaction should be positive only. This is definitely challenging for me, but I'm trying it and having some good luck with it.

We are getting closer to a Scott weekend, and that causes a little anxiety, for the kids and me alike. I think it helps that the kids haven't seen him for a month. We'll see how next week goes. Kayla and Ethan do need skills on how to handle their emotions in terms of when they are triggered and what triggers them. We are busy with extracurricular activities, and everyone is excited about the coming summer! Can't believe we have been living in Leon for a year!

May 20, 2016

It was the Friday night of Scott's weekend. The kids went without complaint. Collin and I went out to eat and had a lovely dinner with just the two of us. I did enjoy our weekends alone together. After dinner we went to the water, which we often did. There we fed the fish till it was getting dark.

I was getting a chill and was ready to head back to catch a movie at his house. As we walked back to the car, though, Collin wanted to check out his favorite fishing spot that was just down the path.

"I really like this fishing spot," he commented. It was getting chilly, but I reluctantly went with him, holding his hand. The way the moonlight hit the water was breathtaking. You could see the reflection of the full moon dancing in the ripples. The glow of the water gave the appearance almost of daylight. The effect was beautiful.

I was turning around to put in my protest of wanting to get warm, when there was Collin on the ground. He was down on one knee with his arms up in the air, holding something up to me. He said, "Heather, I love you. Will you marry me?"

Excitement and joy overwhelmed me, along with, for whatever reason, the thought of his being a jokester. Before I could stop myself or even realize what I was saying, "Are you kidding me? Is this a joke?" escaped my lips.

A look of devastation waved across his face. Immediately I exclaimed, "YES, OF COURSE!"

We hugged and kissed. Collin slipped the ring onto my finger. It was stunning. We were both ecstatic about this new chapter that we would be embarking on.

"Are you sure you're ready to take on my circus?"

"Absolutely. I love those kids. And I love you."

How blessed am I to have him?

As we walked hand-in-hand back to the car, where it was warm, Collin repeated, "Are you kidding? Is this a joke?"

I had completely forgotten I had said that.

"I'm so sorry. I didn't even realize I had said it. I was just in so much shock!"

"I thought, 'Uh oh, I made a mistake. She doesn't want this.'"

"Oh no! I do!"

"It's okay—it makes for a great story!" *Oh, goodie!*

May 22, 2016

When the kids got home Sunday we ordered pizza. We sat outside at our table and chairs.

"Collin and I have decided that we don't want to date anymore," I announced matter-of-factly, watching the expressions playing across their faces.

"We're going to get married instead!" I finished immediately, not wanting to prolong their pain or confusion.

"WOW! Don't tell me things like that. I almost had a heart attack, thinking you were breaking up!" Kayla exclaimed.

All three kids were really excited and started dancing around.

I know what you are thinking as you read this: "Thought you said you weren't going to get married again." I truly believed God was gifting me with Collin.

Yes, I had thought that with Scott, but I had married him out of obligation. I had felt that I needed to take care of him. I was truly in love with Collin. I believed, and still believe, that he is my soulmate and the only one I am supposed to be with.

From My Journaling May 12, 2015 (a year earlier)

If I do find another man, I need him to be a strong follower of God. Walk The Walk, not just talk the talk. You will have to be patient, kind, comforting, and someone who can listen to me and not try to fix me. Just be by my side through life, helping us grow closer to God. He has to put God before me. This guy does not exist. He would have to be Jesus . . . Even before thinking of dating again, this new guy would have to impress my kids, be a good role model for Ethan, and be supportive.

I can't believe Collin does exist! I am so very happy.

CHAPTER 52

Expressed Concerns and Fun with Words

Journal Entry: May 27, 2006

We're only a few days into our engagement, and I'm on the receiving end of concerns from someone that I'm moving too fast and that we only want a baby. I understand where they're coming from. I feel a little hurt that they think I'm wanting to replace the kids. I'm sorry that it looks as though a baby is our main concern.

I have said that if Collin wants more kids we had better get a move on due to my age. However, the reality is more of "If it happens, it happens—if it doesn't, it doesn't." I thanked this person for bringing this concern to my attention and will try not to give that impression.

Our main concern is setting an example for the kids. We want to show them what a relationship is supposed to look like—with love, kindness, support, and encouragement. We are ready to move on and take the next step of moving in together and staying together forever.

We are both old fashioned, so we agreed to set the example of wanting to get married. I know that the girls know not to rely on a man or have kids as a panacea for unhappiness. We have discussed this multiple times. I have seen Kayla have a boyfriend and recently kick him to the curb because he was flirting with his "old girlfriend," so she didn't want anything further to do with him.

Erica has boys falling at her feet because she is so pretty, and she just says, in so many words, "whatever—not interested." We talk about having babies and how expensive and time-consuming they are. We talk about how this would affect their future. Both girls have career goals, and both know that it would be more difficult to accomplish them with a child. I actually think having a baby in the house would reinforce this for them.

The person who offered the unsolicited advice also pointed out a fear that I would treat a biological child differently from the others. It is true that parents treat their individual children differently. It's because they have to. Each child is unique and has to be loved uniquely—not more or less than any other, but differently.

I didn't know this variation existed when I first had the kids move in. It took a few months, but as I fell in love with each child I realized that I loved each one in a special way. Differently, based on their needs and personalities.

I used to feel that there had been favoritism from my parents, but my kids have taught me that this was only my perception. It can feel like that from a kid's point of view, but as a parent you are really loving all your kids equally—just in different ways.

June 13, 2016

Summer had officially kicked off. I couldn't believe Erica was going to be a freshman in the fall. She would be working at the pool for the summer and had made the dance team! That would keep her busy the entire school year. She still played the flute and had made lots of friends! She would also be in Future Farmers of America in the fall, so we would see if she liked that! She was really an independent young lady, and I couldn't believe how much she had grown.

Kayla was in 4H and loving it! She would be in the seventh grade. She would be showing Odin at the fair during the summer. She also had made a lot of friends and was getting invited to numerous activities. She played the clarinet and enjoyed it. She was also in choir. She wasn't much of an athlete but wanted to try track next year and possibly softball the following summer. Kayla would be doing some babysitting during the summer to keep her occupied.

She continued to have a lot of emotional issues, though. Little things would set her off. Her psychologist said it would take time and lots of counseling. Brenda was still working with her a lot and suspected there might be other underlying issues we had yet to explore. Kayla was having really good and really bad days, and we continually said prayers for her. I kept trying to rely on God, but there were definitely days when I wasn't sure where He was.

Ethan was in baseball during the summer and would be rotating to football in the fall and basketball in the winter. Phew. He would be in the fifth grade in the fall. He was also playing the tuba!! The instrument was as big as he was! He had made one good friend but continued to be the kid who fit into every group and just bounced around. He would be home alone during the summer but would enjoy the pool and parks. He had already complained about how long the summer had already been, and it had just started! Ethan had moments yet, too, of being set off, but his current issues paled in comparison to Kayla's.

The kids continued to be compelled to see Scott every other weekend. The planned once-a-month visits with him had happened only once. I still have documentation to state that he shouldn't be with the kids and that it would be unhealthy for them emotionally when we went back to mediation in September.

I was really hoping that, in light of my relationship with Collin and our recent engagement, Scott would start backing off. The kids were getting busy with their own events and activities and were increasingly involved in events happening on weekends. On "his" weekends they would hang out with his family, and family members would take care of the kids most of the time. The kids at least enjoyed his family's company.

Collin and I were busy with our wedding plans for September! We had decided to move forward soon to increase stability and security for the kids. Everything was coming together nicely.

Collin was like a bridezilla in that he wanted a big wedding with lots of people, but I preferred something really simple. So we compromised—still simple, but a lot of people invited.

Collin's family were getting a kick out of telling people we were getting married.

When people asked Marie who it was Collin was marrying, she tried her best to explain to people how we had met.

"NO, we are not inbreeding!" Marie would assure people a lot.

Collin's favorite way to tell people: "Remember those three cousins we had stay with us a few years ago?"

He'd wait for them to answer and then hit them with, "I'm marrying their mom!"

He loved their reactions when they started to believe that Collin was about to marry a cousin!

CHAPTER 53

The Park Incident

August 19, 2016

We decided to try a different psychiatrist for Kayla to see whether there could be a different approach than the one she was on. Things were still not going well for her, and we seemed to be stuck. Dr. Kinn came highly recommended by someone I trusted, and he was in much closer proximity and thus more easily accessible than her earlier psychiatrist. He started her on Zoloft and was increasing her meds but would be trying to take her off Abilify.

Kayla continued to experience a breakdown about once a week and was starting to have panic attacks. She claimed that she had problems only with me and that she didn't love me, didn't need me, and didn't want to live with me. I saw her have such breakdowns with Collin, though, too.

Any time she received constructive criticism, was told what to do, or was forced to deal in any way with

261

authority, she would lose it. We had gone so far as to try treating those approaches like a supervisor sandwich— one good thing, the issue or behavior that needed to be addressed or improved, followed up or covered by another good one. Kayla claimed that all I do is yell. The truth is that I have yelled after she has pushed every last button and even told me to go fuck myself. That's when I've yelled!

Last night there was an upset when the girls were five minutes past curfew coming back from the park. Then there were boys over to the house shortly afterward, which explained why they had been late from the park. I never yelled, never raised my voice. Just plain stated facts. They got a consequence of every minute late corresponding to a dollar off their allowance.

Erica took it well, knowing that what she had done was wrong. Kayla proceeded with her usual backtalk, which I ignored. I would try to approach her later, knowing she would hang onto her grievance for a few days. Dr. Kinn diagnosed anxiety and depression, but I still truly believed there was more.

Erica had boys crushing on her, so we talked again after the incident about not allowing herself to be used, having respect for herself, and making sure she maintained boundaries. I did realize that she was still grappling with issues that bothered her, but she never wanted to talk about them and didn't want to continue seeing Brenda.

"Counselors don't help. I don't want to talk to anyone about it because I can take care of it myself," she declared. I was getting little tidbits here and there about her thoughts.

"I worry about making mistakes and turning into Stacy," Erica confided in me.

"Oh, no, Honey. You are very responsible and make good decisions. You are so caring and kind. You will end up making mistakes, but everyone makes mistakes. No one is perfect. The key is learning from your mistakes."

She then told me about a dream she had experienced twice.

"I dream that Scott touches me inappropriately. I wake up with my pants off. I don't like the way he looks at me. He tries to tickle me in my armpit but always manages to brush against my chest."

"Hmmm, we will have to keep an eye on that."

I didn't know what to think about this. A long time ago I had been concerned about the way he had hugged her. However, sometimes she could be overdramatic—being fifteen and all.

Erica proceeded to tell me how concerned she was about Kayla.

"I don't think Kayla is well."

"Oh, why is that?"

"Kayla wants to run away so that it scares you and Collin."

"Oh?"

"Yeah, we were talking to Becky and she has been through some tough times *("she" being the cousin who had attempted suicide)*. Becky was telling Kayla how to run away without getting into trouble."

"Really? Like what?"

"Like don't be gone for over twenty-four hours—and she was encouraging Kayla to do it."

"WHY? Why does Kayla want to run away?"

"Kayla has always hated you. Kayla is just using you. Her calling you Mom is just a ploy. Kayla has always been angry at you and just fakes it."

I did believe this. Kayla was really good at manipulating and using people. I watched her do it to Scott all the time. She would tell everyone else how much she hated him, yet use him for money. She had even told me, "Hey, it's saving you money." I was afraid that Kayla was still traveling down a dark path of destruction and could and would manipulate people to get what she wanted. I wished I had known what to do.

CHAPTER 54

The Big Day

August 22, 2016

Collin sold his house in Osceola and moved in with us in Leon. We decided to keep the kids in the same school district rather than uproot them.

"We won't have to move again until you graduate!" I told the kids.

Someday we hope to move back to Osceola. Collin would like to take over his family farm one day. I would love that, getting back to the country!

Collin and I were getting married in just a few weeks. The kids were excited—at least they acted like it. I was excited about getting back into a routine the following week, too, with school starting. I had been hoping that once Collin had moved in we could concentrate on becoming a family with a routine and set a good example of how a family is supposed to operate. Maybe things would settle down.

August 27, 2016

We were finishing up final wedding plans! Everyone was excited! Kayla loved helping with the wedding and was very good at it. She is a great decorator and planner. Kayla had been doing exceptionally well on her new medication, and I was very hopeful that we were reforming! Maybe we had found the right medication with the right psychiatrist . . . finally.

Collin had been a huge help. We were settling down into a nice routine, and the last few days had been wonderful! I was very hopeful about our new life. Erica started high school and started seeing the boy she had met at the park the night she and Kayla had been late coming home. I wasn't so sure about this boy, Blake, yet. There was something about him that seemed strange, but I couldn't quite put my finger on it yet.

"Mom, can he come to the wedding?" Erica asked. "It would probably be just the dance."

"Sure, I don't see why not. Maybe we can visit with him and get to know him better."

"I don't know. He's really shy,"

September 4, 2016

The big day had arrived! Our house was abuzz with the women getting ready. The bridesmaids and mothers got ready at our house. People came and went all morning, getting hair and makeup done.

We met the guys at the church for pictures before the ceremony. Behind the church is an elegant flower garden with a path and a wooden bridge. Collin stood on the bridge with his back to me. I walked up behind him and placed my hand on his shoulder. He turned around, and we looked into each other's eyes for the first time on our wedding day. His face lit up when he saw me in my wedding dress. I found him to be very appealing in his tuxedo.

Kelly took our pictures. She did a wonderful job coming up with different positions in which to place people and explaining where she wanted everyone to stand. Megan was also there. It was nice to have them in attendance, as they are still good friends of mine. They have helped the kids so much during visits with Scott.

The ceremony went off without a hitch. During the unity candle section we did something special. We had a jar that had a family tree with all of our names on it. We each had our own smaller jar, into which we placed our own, uniquely colored sand. We poured our colored sand from our private jars as we filled up the family jar. Each color symbolized one of us individually, but as our sand blended it made a beautiful picture in the family jar.

As we did this Kayla cried. It touched my heart to see her well up with tears (hopefully of joy) and made me hopeful that she would remain excited and happy about this new excursion. When we were done creating our masterpiece, we joined hands in a circle as the pastor blessed our new family. Again Kayla cried. She had so many tears that Ethan and Erica were staring at her. Poor Kayla, overcome with so much emotion!

The reception had a couple of hiccups, but nothing we couldn't fix. Collin gave a thank you speech and, of course, started it off with, "How many people came today thinking: Are you kidding me? Is this a joke?"

He was referring to his actually getting married, being that he had never come out of the woods or left the farm prior to his relationship with me. He finished the thought with a playful jab at me for saying those words when he asked me to marry him.

Erica gave a speech she had worked very hard on. It was a very touching speech about being a family and how we had always been there for her. It made me cry. She did a great job of speaking in front of a couple hundred people.

Ethan sang a song that Collin's uncle had helped him create: "I'm so happy, I'm so glad . . . Collin's my cousin, and now my dad." It made everyone laugh!

Kayla sang a solo in front of everyone! She sang it karaoke style, and her voice was stunning. I really hope she pursues singing!

The dance was fun, and everyone had a great time! Hugs were shared, laughter exchanged, and there were smiles all around. Erica's boyfriend showed up for the dance. He didn't want to come into the hall, being that there were so many people and he was shy.

I went outside and exchanged pleasantries with him. I had a couple drinks in me by then but kept my composure, not wanting to grill him about his intentions with my daughter. Being that this was my night, I kept it short but got to talk to him briefly. He seemed very shy, almost intimidated; yet there was still an uneasy feeling in the pit of my stomach.

At the end of the night we were helping to clean up and trying to round up kids to get them to the places they needed to go. When we went outside we were surprised to find Erica's boyfriend still there, waiting for a ride. We sent Erica and the kids with my parents but waited there for a few minutes with him for his ride. We offered to give him a lift to where he needed to go, but he insisted that his dad was almost there.

His dad pulled up and he got in. There was something I didn't like. Was he scared of his dad? I found Blake to be very shy and intimidated. I decided not to worry about this at this time; after all, it was my wedding night!

The next day we were back at our house opening presents. Our parents, Collin's and my siblings, and the kids were here enjoying the day. We watched the raw footage from the video my uncle had composed for us the previous night.

I noticed at the beginning of the ceremony that Kayla was already crying. We got to the part where the unity sand was being poured, and I watch her cry continuously. It looked as though they weren't tears of joy, though, but of sadness. I continued to watch Kayla throughout the rest of the ceremony. They were definitely tears of sadness, loss, or even grief. Troubled, I decided not to dwell on this, at least for the time being.

As the day was coming to a close, the busy hum of the house and laughter of all my family made me reflect on how far we had come. I was absolutely amazed at God and how He works in mysterious ways.

I am in awe of how God used Scott to pull me out of my partying days. Later, I asked for something more in life, so God used my family's car accident to bring the kids and us together. God worked through the kids, who endured tragic situations, and helped them show me the strength to change our life course. If it hadn't been for the kids, I would have stayed in my situation with Scott.

Finally, God used the kids' lives to introduce me to my true soulmate, Collin. How blessed I am! God is in control of everything that happens, even when we don't understand. His sovereign power can clearly be seen. I thought I was going to save the kids, but in reality they saved me.

Made in the USA
Coppell, TX
08 March 2021